Passing the
Oxbridge Admissions Tests

Second edition

Passing the
Oxbridge Admissions Tests

Rosalie Hutton and Glenn Hutton

Second edition

Learning Matters
An imprint of SAGE Publications Ltd
1 Oliver's Yard
55 City Road
London EC1Y 1SP

SAGE Publications Inc
2455 Teller Road
Thousand Oaks, California 91320

SAGE Publications India PVT LTD
B1/I 1 Mohan Cooperative Industrial Area
Malthura Road
New Delhi 110 044

SAGE Publications Asia-Pacific Pte Ltd
3 Church Street
#10-04 Samsung Hub
Singapore 049483

Editor: Amy Thornton
Development Editor: Jennifer Clark
Production Controller: Chris Marke
Project Management: Swales & Willis Ltd,
Exeter, Devon
Marketing Manager: Catherine Slinn
Cover Design: Wendy Scott
Typeset by: Swales & Willis Ltd, Exeter, Devon
Printed by: TJ International Ltd, Padstow, Cornwall

© 2008, 2012 Rosalie Hutton and Glenn Hutton

First published in 2008
Second edition published in 2012

Library of Congress Control Number: 2012938957

British Library Cataloguing in Publication Data

A catalogue record for this book is available from the British Library

ISBN: 978 0 85725 872 4
ISBN: 978 0 85725 797 0 (pbk)

Contents

Preface

The University of Cambridge researched and developed the Thinking Skills Assessment (TSA), which has been in use since 2001, when the demand for some of their courses far outweighed availability and the fact that there were an ever-increasing number of applicants with high grades at A-level. This demand has not changed with Cambridge receiving 16,000 applications in 2011 and offering 3,400 students places. The courses using the TSA at Cambridge include Computer Science, Economics, Engineering, Land Economy, Natural Sciences (Physical), Natural Sciences (Biological), Philosophy and Social and Political Sciences. This is not a definitive list and the college applied for will inform applicants whether the TSA is an admissions requirement. Cambridge also uses the Biomedical Admissions Test (BMAT) for entry to study medicine and has two subject-specific admissions tests, the Sixth Term Examination Paper (Mathematics) and the Cambridge Law Test.

The University of Oxford has experienced similar issues to Cambridge and in 2011 offered just 3,200 of its 17,000 applicants places. It also uses the TSA (Oxford) for applicants to undergraduate courses in Philosophy, Politics and Economics, Economics and Management and Experimental Psychology or Psychology and Philosophy. In addition to the TSA (Oxford) use is made of other admissions tests including the National Admissions Test for Law (LNAT), the United Kingdom Clinical Aptitude Test (UKCAT) and the Biomedical Admissions Test (BMAT). Several other tests are also used either at the interview stage or before, for example, Mathematics Aptitude Test, Physics Aptitude Test and the History Aptitude Test. All the tests, including the Cambridge tests, are discussed in Chapter 6.

The admissions tests for Oxford and Cambridge are designed to help admissions tutors to determine whether candidates have the skills and aptitudes that are required to study for their chosen degree, for example, the ability to think critically, reason analytically, and use language accurately and effectively.

Research has examined the predictive validity of the TSA for first-year examination performance in Computer Science, Economics, Engineering, and Natural Sciences at the University of Cambridge. The research used three successive years of TSA and examination data. The findings indicated that the total scores of the TSA were a strong predictor of achieving both the highest and the lowest examination classes (*The predictive validity of the Thinking Skills Assessment: a combined analysis of three cohorts*, Joanne L. Emery, October

2007). This is reassuring in the sense that the tests do appear to be achieving their intended purpose.

The purpose of this book is essentially to provide a step-by-step guide to understanding critical-reasoning tests, problem-solving tests, and the elements of Oxford's Writing Task.

This book is the third in a series where universities have introduced pre-entry assessments in order to discriminate amongst applicants. The two previous books are concerned with the UK Clinical Aptitude Test (UKCAT) and Biomedical Admissions Test (BMAT), and the National Admissions Test for Law (LNAT). The UKCAT/BMAT is a test required for those applying to study medicine or dentistry, whilst the LNAT is for applicants intending to study law. Both these tests are discussed briefly in Chapter 6 of this book.

About the authors

Rosalie Hutton is an Occupational Psychologist, specialising in the field of assessment and testing, who designs and publishes a range of psychological assessment measures. Critical-reasoning and problem-solving tests have been used commercially for a number of years in the recruitment and selection of staff and Rosalie provides the rationale for the use of these tests together with a developmental approach to understanding critical-reasoning and problem-solving type questions and how best to arrive at the correct answer. Rosalie is also the co-author of the other two books in this series.

Glenn Hutton has worked at a senior level in a major assessment organisation that tests several thousand people a year using multiple-choice type questions. During this time he had close links with the National Board of Medical Examiners in the United States which tests up to 100,000 doctors a year using online multiple-choice tests. Glenn is also a technical author for Oxford University Press annually producing manuals associated with criminal law, and is co-author of the two other books in this series.

Chapter 1
Introduction

1. Oxbridge admissions tests

Both Oxford and Cambridge use the Thinking Skills Assessment (TSA) and Oxford also includes a second element where candidates are required to undertake a Writing Task.

The TSA results are not used in isolation and both universities consider other information available about each candidate including GCSE results and other qualifications, predicted grades for A-Level or equivalent, school reference, UCAS personal statement, samples of school work and interview performance, to assess potential and select applicants.

At Cambridge the TSA is taken at the time of interview in the UK and overseas and is administered under examination conditions with an invigilator present. Applicants do not need to do anything in terms of registering for the test as Cambridge colleges will notify applicants of all admissions requirements.

To find out whether you will need to take the TSA at Oxford or Cambridge you are advised to look at the exact entry requirements for a particular course by referring to the University of Oxford and University of Cambridge websites.

2. How will this book help me?

This book has been produced to provide any person preparing for the TSA with an in-depth understanding of the assessment they will face.

Chapter 1 of the book examines your choice of applying to Oxford or Cambridge and the admissions process to these universities. The process outlined is simply a summary and is not intended to replace the informative websites provided by the universities (Oxford: www.ox.ac.uk; Cambridge: www.cam.ac.uk), or the *UCAS Big Guide*. This UCAS book is really a **MUST** for any applicant, being the official universities and colleges entrance guide. There are also a useful number of publications available about the entrance to Oxbridge and details are on the universities' websites.

Chapter 2 provides full details of the TSA requirements. This is followed by a clear explanation of the format and design of multiple-choice questions both generally and specific to the TSA.

Chapter 3 provides a step-by-step, developmental approach to answering problem-solving and critical-thinking questions. By the end of this chapter you should have a good understanding of this type of assessment and how best to arrive at the correct answer.

Chapter 4 replicates the Thinking Skills Assessment. The chapter consists of 50 questions – 25 problem solving and 25 critical thinking. In the actual test the time allowed is 90 minutes and you might consider timing yourself against this constraint for some indication as to your level of performance. However, this practice test has not been written to be time constrained but as a vehicle: (a) to consolidate what has been learnt from the previous chapter, and (b) to give you confidence when dealing with such questions. Rather than simply giving the 'correct response', the answers to the practice test provide the rationale for both the correct and incorrect answers. This approach has proved to be effective in developing a person's knowledge and understanding of a particular subject.

Chapter 5 looks at the Writing Task requirement used by Oxford. This is not meant to be an exhaustive review of the skills required for this task but does consider style, structure, and the use of critical-thinking skills, to enable you to write a well-reasoned piece of work in the time allowed.

Chapter 6 examines the other admissions tests used by Oxford and Cambridge.

In addition to the practice tests and information given here, there are other things that can be done to prepare for your admission to Oxford or Cambridge. Whilst it may seem very informal, one of the most effective ways, both to prepare for and succeed in your interview and study in higher education, is to read a 'quality' newspaper. In fact the universities recommend this.

This book does not claim to be able to help you do well in the test but it should speed up your reactions and give you confidence in the style of questions you will encounter.

3. Application process for Oxford and Cambridge

The application process for Oxford and Cambridge starts earlier than other universities. Your UCAS application must usually be submitted by **mid-October** for entry the following year or deferred entry the year after, so that there is time to arrange the interview process. UCAS accept applications from the beginning of **September**.

For Oxford you will also need to complete an Oxford Application Form, and return it to the Undergraduate Admissions Office by post by **mid-October**. The application deadlines and admissions test arrangements may be different for candidates applying from outside the EU.

In the past all applicants to Cambridge were asked to submit a Cambridge Application Form in addition to a UCAS application. It is planned that applicants from the UK and EU will only need to submit a UCAS application in order to apply to Cambridge. If you are applying from outside the EU, you will need to submit a Cambridge Overseas Application Form (COAF) in addition to your UCAS application. However, once your application has been received you will be asked to provide additional information through a Supplementary Application Questionnaire (SAQ).

Both Oxford and Cambridge, depending on your intended course of study, may require you to provide one or two samples of academic work for tutors to assess.

Also, you may already know this, but if you don't, you cannot apply to Oxford and Cambridge in the same year.

Educational requirements

Oxford

Conditional offers are made to students studying A-levels and will range between A*A*A* and AAA depending on the subject applied for. These offers are likely to be on the basis of final grades alone and not UMS scores. The actual requirements are detailed on the Oxford website. With the exception of General Studies, all A-levels are approved for admissions purposes providing that any specific subject requirements are met. Where AS module grades or marks are provided within the UCAS application this information may be used by tutors in considering an applicant's academic attainment up to that point but the information is not used to shortlist for interview.

Applicants must also have sufficient fluency in written and spoken English to cope with their course from the start. Therefore, all non-native English-speaking applicants must hold one of the following qualifications: IELTS; TOEFL (paper-based or internet-based); Cambridge Certificate of Advanced English; Cambridge Certificate for Proficiency in English; English Language GCSE; IGCSE or O-level; International Baccalaureate Standard Level; European Baccalaureate. Applicants must reach a standard set by Oxford in one of these qualifications.

Cambridge

Prior knowledge of certain subjects is required for many courses at Cambridge and conditional offers are made to applicants who pass such subjects with an A or A* grade at A-Level. There are some courses that do not require applicants to have previously studied the subject such as Law, Philosophy and Asian and Middle Eastern Studies. You are recommended to look at the course requirements provided on the website to be aware what subjects and combination of subjects are necessary for your intended course.

As with Oxford, there is also a requirement that an applicant's English language skills are good enough for you to undertake their studies. This may require a formal English language qualification as part of a conditional offer and these qualifications are similar to those required by Oxford.

Writing your personal statement

Before offering a place, Oxford and Cambridge are looking at three main things: your exam results, your referee's statement and your personal statement. Exam results and referees' statements seldom help universities to make selection decisions, whereas the personal statement is your opportunity to convince the university to offer you a place. They want to see that you will fit into university life, not just academically but socially as well.

Apart from telling the reader of your personal statement why you want to study at Oxford or Cambridge you should also include information about your work experience, volunteer work, academic commitment and extracurricular activities.

Work experience can often be difficult for those of you who are coming straight from full-time education but access schemes at weekends and during holidays are often available especially in the A2 year. However, do not be dismayed if you have problems gaining work experience; universities are aware of how difficult this can be.

Volunteer work is considered by many as important in the sense that it demonstrates a commitment to helping others in the community and develops your people and softer skills. Getting involved is easy and you should look for something you would enjoy and that you might stick at for months or longer. Lots of volunteering positions only require up to four hours commitment a week and with some there are opportunities to attend training courses, e.g. first aid. Careers advisers may be able to help organise volunteer work or you can visit the following websites: www.volunteering.org.uk (this is the Volunteering England site and contains information and addresses); www.do-it.org.uk (this is 'volunteering made easy'; just enter your address and the type of project you want to get involved with). So if you aren't volunteering you might consider it's time to get off your bum and start to help others – oh and by the way, it can be FUN and it's FREE!

Academic commitment means demonstrating that you understand the commitment required for the hard work you will face to complete your degree and beyond. Your exam results do not amply demonstrate your commitment to studying, but reading up on an area of your intended degree that might interest you would – so make a note of everything you read outside your A-level course work in preparation for completing the personal statement.

Extra-curricular activities are important as these provide evidence that you are a well-rounded person with a number of hobbies and interests. This may include playing representative sport, being a member of a society, a musician, or undertaking the Duke of Edinburgh Awards scheme. Where possible showing positions of responsibility is beneficial to demonstrate your leadership skills and the fact that you are confident and willing to undertake such responsibilities.

Be mindful that at least 80 per cent of your personal statement should relate to your academic studies, with only a small paragraph devoted to extra-curricular activities. The university is selecting suitable applicants from a significant number of very high achievers and is really concerned with how successfully you will cope with the demanding courses. The aim of your personal statement is to impress upon the admissions tutor that you are academically able, intellectually curious, enthusiastic and hardworking.

Because of the nature of the beast, in so far as its importance at this point in the application process, the personal statement has become more and more 'professional' in its production. As a result Oxbridge often put the statements through plagiarism detection software and apparently many have been failed. Be warned!

Essentially your personal statement is the opportunity to convince the course tutor of your strong academic background, a genuine interest in your chosen subject and a self-motivated and enthusiastic approach.

Interviews

The Oxford and Cambridge websites contain detailed information on interviews, what to expect, how to prepare and even what to wear. Consequently, the following provides just a basic outline of the interview process. Remember, the interview is just one aspect of your application, as tutors will also consider your examination results, personal statement, academic reference, predicted grades, and admissions tests or written work (where required).

The interview is designed to assess your academic abilities and, most importantly, your academic potential. It not only provides tutors with an opportunity to evaluate your understanding of, and aptitude for, your subject, but also gives you the opportunity to explain why you are committed to your proposed course of study. It is important to note that whether or not you are accepted will be based on your academic abilities and potential, not your manners or etiquette, appearance, or background.

In a nutshell you will be required to demonstrate your:

- academic ability
- capacity to deal with the rigours of the course
- logic and reasoning ability
- knowledge of current affairs, especially those concerning the course.

These areas are really what you would expect, and the last point reiterates the benefits of reading around your chosen subject by regularly reading a 'quality' newspaper, journals, magazines and other relevant publications.

4. *Thinking Skills Assessment*

The Thinking Skills Assessment (TSA) is designed to help Oxford and Cambridge to make more informed choices amongst the many highly qualified applicants who apply for some of their degree programmes. The test has been designed to assess the ability of individuals to think critically and reason analytically, traits that identify individuals who are most likely to succeed in higher education.

The TSA is an assessment of two kinds of thinking: problem solving – reasoning using numerical and spatial skills, and critical thinking – reasoning using everyday written language.

The assessment consists of 50 multiple-choice questions within a time constraint of 90 minutes. The test is normally pencil and paper, although facilities do exist for it to be conducted online. Where the test is pencil and paper a soft pencil (HB or softer) and a good eraser are essential. All of the 50 questions must be attempted and these vary in difficulty from easy to very hard. There are 25 problem-solving questions and 25 critical-thinking questions that are mixed throughout the question paper. The reason for this is to ensure candidates complete a sufficient number of each type of question should they not complete the full test in the time allotted. It is recommended that candidates work steadily through the test from start to finish rather than jump around. Calculators are NOT permitted, but dictionaries (book or electronic) are, although this provision is primarily aimed at candidates whose first language is not English.

The additional Writing Task required by Oxford is allocated 30 minutes and candidates are provided with three essay questions from which they select one. The essay questions are on general subjects that do not require any specialised knowledge. The purpose of the Writing Task is to afford candidates an opportunity to show that they can communicate effectively in writing, organising their ideas and presenting them clearly and concisely.

In relation to the problem-solving element of the TSA a curriculum is provided by Cambridge Assessment and this is reproduced in Chapter 3.

Chapter 2
Multiple-choice questions

In respect of the critical-thinking element of the TSA, designers of similar tests, e.g. UKCAT/BMAT and LNAT, will maintain that the tests do not contain any curriculum, nor any science content, nor can it be revised for. Tests like the UKCAT and LNAT, together with the critical-thinking element of the test being presented by Cambridge Assessment, have been in existence for many decades and are used widely in the selection, assessment and development of staff. None of these commercially available tests claims to have any curriculum or science content and cannot specifically be revised for. However, it has been demonstrated that familiarisation in understanding and practising such tests does increase both levels of competence and performance. It also helps to reduce anxiety levels as applicants are not faced with the unknown.

5. Format and design of multiple-choice questions

This section provides a brief overview of multiple-choice question tests and then examines their format and design and in particular that being used in the TSA.

Which of the following is true of multiple-choice tests and questions?

A The tests are very simplistic

B The questions are easy to answer

C The tests are a poor substitute for real examinations

D A good guessing strategy will always get you a decent mark

E None of the above

The answer, of course, is E – none of the above.

Multiple-choice tests have a very good track record in the field of assessment and particularly in selection. Multiple-choice questions offer a technique that simply tests the candidates' knowledge and understanding of a particular subject on the date of the test. They make candidates read and think but *not write* about the question set, as is the case with essay-type questions.

It is true that there have been a number of long-held criticisms – and myths – about multiple-choice tests. For one, it has been a criticism that they are too simple-minded and trivial. What this observation really means is that it is perfectly obvious to the candidate what they have to do. There are no marks for working out what the examiner wants – it's obvious. But this is not the same as saying that the *answer* is obvious, far from it. In addition, multiple-choice questions are often referred to by students as being 'multiple-guess' questions, on the basis that the right answer lies in one of the options given and therefore you have a good mathematical chance of happening upon the right answer. Although systematic and even completely random guessing does occur in multiple-choice tests, their effects can be minimised and their use identified by properly constructed, presented and timed tests. The people who design and analyse multiple-choice tests are often just as interested in what *wrong* answers you give as the right ones. This is because, apart from other things, patterns can be discerned and compared with those of others taking the same test and tendencies towards certain answers (e.g. always choosing option B) will stand out.

In short, guessing is easy to spot and unlikely to succeed. Given that the purpose of the TSA is to inform the overall decision-making process in selecting you over your fellow applicants (rather than simply achieving a bad result or score) relying on guesswork is a poor strategy.

Multiple-choice tests are used extensively both in Europe and the USA, from staged tests in schools through to university selection and assessment, to some of the most complex and high-stake professional trade qualifications.

The strength of these tests is that they can provide fair and objective testing on a huge scale at small cost, in the sense that their administration is standardised and their developers can demonstrate that the results are not going to vary according to the marker, a criticism of essay-type tests.

The format and design of the multiple-choice questions used for the TSA will undoubtedly follow the general educational model.

The following descriptions of the format and design of multiple-choice questions are taken from two publications. First, *Assessment and Testing: A survey of research* (University of Cambridge Local Examinations Syndicate, 1995). The University of Cambridge Local Examinations Syndicate has been in existence for well over 100 years and prepares examinations for over 100 countries. Second, *Constructing Written Test Questions for the Basic Clinical Sciences* (Second Edition, Susan M Case and David B Swanson, National Board of Medical Examiners, 1998). The National Board of Medical Examiners, which is based in the USA, uses multiple-choice questions to test in excess of 100,000 medical students each year, including foreign doctors, at numerous sites throughout the world.

In all, multiple-choice testing properly conducted is well established, well used across the professional assessment world and well respected, none more so than Cambridge Assessment.

There are a number of different formats that can be used for multiple-choice tests but the most common format is that taken from the 'One Best Answer' family. Generally, this is the format used in the TSA and is discussed in detail below in relation to numerical/spatial tests and critical-thinking tests. However, before looking at the TSA it is useful to understand the general structure of the 'One Best Answer' format.

'One Best Answer' format

The 'One Best Answer' format, also known as A-type questions, are the most widely used in multiple-choice tests. They make explicit the number of choices to be selected and *usually* consist of a *stem*, a *lead-in question*, followed by a series of *choices*, normally between three and five choices. To demonstrate this we will use a simple example taken from a typical numerical aptitude test.

Stem

The *stem* is usually a set of circumstances that can be presented in a number of different ways. The circumstances may be presented in a few simple sentences, as a document, a letter, some form of pictorial display or may be longer passages, such as newspaper articles, extracts from books or periodicals. It provides all the information for the question that will follow.

A simple numerical aptitude *stem* could be:

A college had 20,000 students in 2007. 8,000 of the students studied a science subject.

Lead-in question

The *lead-in question* identifies the exact answer the examiner requires from the circumstances provided in the *stem*.

For example, the *lead-in question* for the *stem* example given above could be:

What is the approximate ratio of students studying science to the total number of students at the college?

Choices

The *choices* provided will always consist of ONE correct answer with the remainder being incorrect answers; these incorrect answers are referred to as 'distracters'.

For example, typical *choices* for the *stem* and *lead-in question* example given above could be:

A 2:3

B 2:5

C 3:2

D 3:5

E 4:2

Answer and rationale

Ratio: rule

A **ratio** allows one quantity to be compared with another quantity. Any two numbers can be compared by writing them alongside each other with the numbers being separated by a ratio sign (:).

Answer: B is correct – 2:5

Step 1: write the figures separated by the ratio sign with the number being compared first, so here 8,000:20,000

Step 2: reduce these figures down if possible. Here they can be reduced to 8:20 by discounting the thousands and then further reduced by dividing both numbers by 4 to obtain 2:5.

Step 3: the ratio of students studying science compared with the total number of students at the college is 2:5.

The areas being tested by the TSA, problem solving and critical thinking, are dealt with separately in Chapter 3.

6. Format of the Thinking Skills Assessment: problem solving

This part of the test assesses your ability to solve numerical and spatial problems. The format is very similar to that described in the numerical aptitude example given above.

Stem

The *stem* will consist of tables, charts, and/or graphs.

Lead-in question

For each of the stems, i.e. the tables, charts, and/or graphs, there will be one *lead-in question*.

Choices

There will be five *choices* for each question, A, B, C, D and E. Remember, there is only ONE correct answer and the remaining four choices will be 'distracters', i.e. incorrect.

7. Format of the Thinking Skills Assessment: critical thinking

This part of the test assesses your ability to think logically about written information and arrive at a reasoned conclusion.

The format of the critical-thinking part of the test is similar to that described in the example given above, with the exception being that the *lead-in question* actually becomes a *statement*. This is explained further in Chapter 3.

Stem

The *stem* will consist of short passages of text.

Lead-in question

For each of the stems, i.e. the passages of text, there will be one *lead-in question*.

Choices

There will be five possible *choices* for each question, A, B, C, D and E. Only ONE of these choices will be the correct answer and the remaining four choices will be 'distracters'.

8. How to approach multiple-choice questions

Whatever the purpose or design of the test, it is worth bearing in mind some general rules to follow when answering multiple-choice questions. Clearly, your score should be higher if you attempt to answer all of the questions in the test and avoid wild guessing. However, if you are running out of time you may attempt some 'educated' guesses but where five options are available this may prove difficult. If there are questions you are unsure of you can return to them later.

Although it is often repeated at every level of testing and assessment in every walk of life, it is nevertheless worth reiterating – **always read the questions carefully**. It may help to read them more than once to avoid misreading a critical word(s).

Where all the options, or some of the options, begin with the same word(s), or appear very similar, be sure to mark the correct option.

When undertaking a multiple-choice test such as the TSA there are essentially two strategies that can be adopted:

Strategy 1

Carefully read the passage, then read each question and then go on to examine each of the options in turn to see whether it is possibly correct or whether it can be eliminated. This process of elimination should leave you with the correct answer. However, you should be aware that you might become more susceptible to the distracters and immediately believe one to be the correct answer. In relation to critical-thinking questions you may then go through a process of 'justifying' your choice to yourself and therefore not have an open mind to conflicting arguments elsewhere in the passage.

This strategy is the more conventional approach that would probably be followed by most test takers.

Strategy 2

Carefully read the passage and then attempt each question *without looking at the options available*. When you have arrived at a possible answer for the question you can examine the options to see if your choice, or a close match, is available. This process would validate or invalidate your answer thus allowing you to move on or review your answer.

Alternatively, you may read the question first and then carefully read the passage in an attempt to arrive at a possible answer before looking at the options.

This is a more deliberate strategy and feels less 'intuitive' than the first strategy above.

It is of course a matter of personal choice which of the two strategies you adopt. However, in either case, an initial skim read of the passage might be beneficial.

In relation to the critical-thinking questions **do not use your own knowledge or experience** of the subject matter to influence your answers even if your knowledge contradicts that of the writer. The concept of this part of the test is not to test individual prior knowledge – it is to present everyone competing against you with the same opportunity to demonstrate their skills and aptitudes. As such your answers should relate directly to:

1. *your understanding of the passage you have read* and
2. *the way in which the writer has presented it to you, the reader.*

Examine each passage to extract the main ideas and avoid drawing hasty conclusions.

The following two chapters of the book contain details of the TSA problem-solving and critical-thinking elements and provides a practice test covering each of these areas. By working through these chapters you will not only familiarise yourself with the format of these tests but speed up your reactions and give yourself the confidence successfully to handle the differing styles of questions involved.

Chapter 3
Thinking Skills Assessment

9. Problem solving

The problem-solving part of the TSA assesses a candidate's ability to solve numerical and spatial problems. It requires the candidate to solve problems by extracting relevant information from tables and other numerical presentations. It assumes familiarity with numbers and a good pass at GCSE but the problems to be solved are less to do with numerical facility and more to do with problem solving (i.e. knowing what information to use and how to manipulate it using simple calculations and ratios). Hence, it measures reasoning using numbers as a vehicle, rather than measuring a facility with numbers.

Commercially-produced numerical aptitude tests have been in existence for many years, mainly for use in the selection and assessment of staff. There have been numerous books written on how to pass or how to master these types of psychometric tests, and what follows is a précis on what you need to consider specifically in approaching this part of the test. Essentially, the advice on preparation for any aptitude test, contained in Chapter 2, holds true for numerical/spatial tests.

Quite simply, numerical and spatial tests are designed to measure your ability to understand numbers and visualise shapes in different dimensions and rotations. The numerical part of the test relates to the four basic arithmetic operations of addition, subtraction, multiplication and division, as well as number sequences and simple mathematics. Therefore, in preparing for such tests you need to be able to perform simple calculations without the use of a calculator.

This chapter provides you with an opportunity to test your understanding and knowledge of the range of numerical and spatial questions you are likely to be presented with in the TSA. By taking this opportunity you should be able to identify any numerical areas where you may need some development. Obviously, as with any other type of examination, numerical questions can be presented in a variety of different ways. However, the basic computations used will always be the same. So learn or remind yourself of the basics! The example questions provided in this chapter not only include the correct answer and rationale but also the reasons why the other options are incorrect. In addition, this section also provides the 'mathematical rule' for each question. All this is designed to reinforce or build on your understanding and knowledge of the syllabus areas.

10. Problem-solving curriculum

Twenty-five of the 50 questions contained in the TSA are numerical/spatial items associated with tables, charts and/or graphs. These questions are mixed with the critical-thinking questions throughout the question paper.

The curriculum for mathematical knowledge and skill, covered in the problem-solving part of the assessment, is provided by Cambridge Assessment (© UCLES 2003) as follows:

Number concepts
- simple fractions
- place value (for example, knowing that the '5' in '7654' indicates '50')
- ideas about percentages (for example, the idea that 1% could be thought of as '1 in every 100', and that if 20% of a group of adults are men, 80% must be women)

Numerical operations
- the four rules of number (addition, subtraction, multiplication, division)
- percentage operations (for example, if something was sold at £10, and is now advertised at '20% off', how much would the customer pay?)
- calculations in everyday contexts (complex calculations with fractions and decimals are not required)

Quantities
- time and the calendar
- money
- measures including:

  length – kilometre (km), metre (m), centimetre (cm), millimetre (mm)

  weight – kilogramme (kg), gramme (g)

  area – square centimetre, square metre

  volume (capacity) – cubic centimetre, litre (l), gallons

Note
Knowledge of the following relationships is also required:

   1 km = 1000 m, 1 m = 100 cm, 1 cm = 10 mm, 1 kg = 1000 g

You are also required to know the terms for measurements that are used informally in daily life (e.g. feet, miles), but numerical relationships for these measures (e.g. 12 inches = 1 foot) are not required.

Space and spatial reasoning
- area (including the calculation of the area of a rectangle)
- perimeter (including calculation)
- volume (including the calculation of the volume of a box)
- reflections (in mirrors) and rotations of simple shapes
- two-dimensional (2D) representations of three-dimensional (3D) shapes (for example, being able to interpret a 'bird's eye view' of a house)

Generalisation
- recognition that some operations are generalisable, for example that converting 24 to 3 and 40 to 5 both involve division by 8 (formal algebra is not required)

Tables and graphs
- extracting information from graphs
- extracting information from tables

Note

The above is the full curriculum that *may* be used in the TSA – because of the limitation in relation to the number of questions in the test (25) not all of the curriculum will be contained in each test.

11. Problem-solving example questions

The type of format used in problem-solving questions is the same as that used as an example of multiple-choice questions in the previous chapter. That is a *stem* in the form of a table, chart or graph, followed by a *lead-in question* and then five possible *choices* – A, B, C, D or E.

Example question

The following example requires you to select the correct answer from the five options provided. The rationale for the correct and incorrect answers is provided after the question.

The table below shows the miles travelled by a sales representative.

	Mon	Tue	Wed	Thu	Fri	Sat
WEEK 1	197.5	189	213.5	231	190	437
WEEK 2	116.5	145	202	173	52	

You want to find her median mileage over the 11 days.

Which of these would you do?

A   Find the sixth number and divide this by 2.

B   Add all the numbers together and divide by 11.

C   Rearrange the numbers into numerical order and then find the sixth number.

D   Find the average for each week and divide this by 2.

E   Add the two middle numbers together and divide this by 2.

Example question: answer and rationale

Median: rule

The **median** of a distribution is the middle value when the values are arranged in order. When there are two middle values (i.e. for an even number of values) then you add the two middle numbers and divide by 2. The highlighted statement and rationale is correct.

A   Find the sixth number and divide this by 2.

This answer is incorrect as the method of finding the median does not entail dividing any of the individual values by 2.

B   Add all the numbers together and divide by 11.

This answer is incorrect as it provides the method for finding the *mean* not the median.

C   Rearrange the numbers into numerical order and then find the sixth number.

This answer is correct.

Step 1: arrange the 11 values in order – so 52, 116.5, 145, 173, 189, 190, 197.5, 202, 213.5, 231, 437.

Step 2: there are an odd number of values, so the median is the middle value, i.e. 190.

D   Find the average for each week and divide this by 2.

This answer is incorrect as it is not a method for finding any type of average.

E   Add the two middle numbers together and divide this by 2.

This answer is incorrect as it provides the method for finding the *median* when dealing with an even number of values.

The questions used by Cambridge Assessment are of three specific kinds: Relevant Selection, Finding Procedures, and Identifying Similarities. Below are three examples, answers and rationale of these types of question.

1. Relevant Selection

Example question

The table below shows the dimensions and prices of various estate cars. I want to buy an estate car for both private and trade use. I am a plumber by trade and need to carry copper pipe in the luggage space up to a length of 1.2 m that for security reasons I want to keep inside the vehicle. I also want to garage my car to prevent it being broken into. My garage is 3.2 m long and 2.25 m wide.

What is the lowest price estate car to satisfy these conditions?

Make	Ford	Peugeot	Fiat	VW
Length	2.8 m	2.5 m	2.6 m	3.25 m
Width	1.48 m	1.36 m	1.38 m	1.50 m
Interior length	1.8 m	1.75 m	1.70 m	2.10 m
Interior width	1.40 m	1.70 m	1.35 m	1.45 m
Luggage space	1.2 m	1.05 m	1.3 m	1.4 m
Private use**	£12,585	£11,995	£12,399	£12,495
Trade use	£10,333	£9,500	£10,459	£10,800

** Private use includes trade use

A   £10,333

B   £10,800

C   £11,995

D   £12,399

E   £12,585

Example question: answer and rationale

'Relevant Selection' means finding the required information from a majority of text that is redundant in achieving the solution, i.e. selecting those parts of the question that are relevant to achieving the correct answer. The highlighted statement and rationale is correct.

A   £10,333

This answer is incorrect as it is the trade price of the Ford and the requirement is a vehicle for private and trade use.

B £10,800

This answer is incorrect as it is the trade price of the VW and the requirement is a vehicle for private and trade use. Also the VW at 3.25 m is too long for the garage at 3.2 m.

C £11,995

This answer is incorrect as the luggage space of the Peugeot at 1.05 m is too small for the copper pipe at 1.2 m.

D £12,399

This answer is correct. We need to find an estate car that will fit in a garage 3.2 m long and 2.25 m wide and which will carry copper pipe in the luggage space up to a length of 1.2 m. The car is for both private and trade use. Both the Fiat and the Ford fit the specifications but the Fiat is cheaper.

E £12,585

This answer is incorrect, as even though the Ford fits all the specifications it is more expensive than the Fiat for private use.

2. Finding Procedures

Example question

Mr Ahmed is replacing his fencing around the perimeter of his house. On the back fence overlooking fields he intends to use three lengths of wooden rails across the total length; on the two sides of the garden two lengths of wooden rails across the total length; on the front garden fence three lengths of wooden rails across the total length. The back fence measures 50 m; each side of the garden measures 45 m; the length of the front garden fence is 48 m which includes a 1 m wide gate. The wooden rails are 3 m long.

How many wooden rails will Mr Ahmed need to undertake all the fencing?

A   127 rails

B   142 rails

C   157 rails

D   158 rails

E   187 rails

Example question: answer and rationale

Multi-stage calculations: rule

'Finding procedures' relates to those occasions when you have abstracted the relevant information but are required to use a method or procedure to find the solution. The highlighted statement and rationale is correct.

A   127 rails

This answer is incorrect as it has used the calculation $45 \times 2 = 90/3 = 30$ rails; it has not doubled the number of rails for the two sides of the garden fence, i.e. $45 \times 2 \times 2 = 180/3 = 60$ rails

B   142 rails

This answer is incorrect as it has multiplied the front garden fence by 2 and not by 3 and has not deducted the 3 m for the gate.

C   157 rails

This answer is correct.

The calculation to arrive at this answer is:

$50 \times 3\ (150) + 45 \times 2\ (90) + 45 \times 2\ (90) + 48 \times 3\ (144) - 3\ (141) = 471$.

Total length = 471 m divided by length of each rail = 471/3 = 157 rails.

D   158 rails

This answer is incorrect as it has failed to deduct the 3 m for the gate in the front garden fence.

E   187 rails

This answer is incorrect as it has multiplied the side fencing of 2×45 m by 3 instead of 2.

3. Identifying Similarities

Example question

Bill is laying a gravel driveway that measures 20 m long and 4 m wide. He has calculated that he will require 0.05 tonnes of 20 mm gravel to cover one square metre of driveway. Bill therefore requires $80 \times 0.05 = 4$ tonnes of gravel.

Which of the following uses the same method of calculation as that above?

A   Sarah is paid £5.25 an hour to clean at the school. She works 3 hours a day for 4 days and 2 hours on Fridays. She earns £73.50 a week.

B To lay a lawn measuring 10.0 m by 6.0 m will require 15 kg of lawn seed where 0.25 kg of seed covers an area of one square metre.

C Lucy puts 60 litres of petrol in her car. The next week she travels 360 miles before the car is empty. Lucy's car does 6 miles to the litre.

D A 5 litre can of paint covers 15 square metres. Ranjit paints a 5.0 m by 4.0 m wall and a 5.0 m by 5.0 m ceiling. Ranjit needs three cans of paint.

E Victor's company car business mileage for June is 1,500 miles and the total mileage is 2,300 miles. His private mileage for June is 800 miles.

Example question: answer and rationale

Identifying Similarities is simply matching the information provided with other information that is similar.

In matching the information provided the procedure multiplies 80 (20 × 4) × 0.05 based on the size of the drive (20 m by 4 m) by the amount of gravel @ 0.05 tonnes per square metre. The highlighted statement and rationale is correct.

A Sarah is paid £5.25 an hour to clean at the school. She works 3 hours a day for 4 days and 2 hours on Fridays. She earns £73.50 a week.

This answer is incorrect as it multiplies (3 × 4) + (3 × 2) × 5.25 thereby using a different procedure, i.e. method of calculation.

B To lay a lawn measuring 10.0 m by 6.0 m will require 15 kg of lawn seed where 0.25 kg of seed covers an area of one square metre.

This answer is correct.

This answer uses the same procedure, i.e. multiplying 60 (10 × 6) by the amount of lawn seed @ 0.25 kg per square metre.

C Lucy puts 60 litres of petrol in her car. The next week she travels 360 miles before the car is empty. Lucy's car does 6 miles to the litre.

This answer is incorrect as it divides 360 by 60 thereby using a different procedure, i.e. method of calculation.

D A 5 litre can of paint covers 15 square metres. Ranjit paints a 5.0 m by 4.0 m wall and a 5.0 m by 5.0 m ceiling. Ranjit needs three cans of paint.

This answer is incorrect as it multiplies 5 × 4 by 5 × 5 and divides by 5 thereby using a different procedure, i.e. method of calculation.

E   Victor's company car business mileage for June is 1,500 miles and the total mileage is 2,300 miles. His private mileage for June is 800 miles.

This answer is incorrect as it subtracts 1,500 from 2,300 thereby using a different procedure, i.e. method of calculation.

12. Critical thinking

The notion that we all have 'thinking skills' or 'core skills' that should be transferable to all subject areas has attracted a great deal of academic interest. One of these 'core skills' is called 'critical thinking' and the vast number of books on the subject testifies to the interest in – and complexity of – the subject. Critical thinking is fundamentally concerned with the way arguments are structured and produced by whatever media; discussion, debate, a paper, a report, an article or an essay. The following are the generally accepted criteria for critical thinking:

- the ability to differentiate between facts and opinions
- the ability to examine assumptions
- being open minded as you search for explanations, causes and solutions
- being aware of valid or invalid argument forms
- staying focused on the whole picture, while examining the specifics
- verifying sources
- deducing and judging inductions
- inducing and judging inductions
- making value judgements
- defining terms and judging definitions
- deciding on actions
- being objective
- a willingness and ability always to look at alternatives

The list above is not meant to be an exhaustive list of all the criteria of critical thinking but it provides an overview of some of the basic principles that underpin the TSA. Applying your own critical reasoning, you will realise at this point that some of the criteria listed will lend themselves more readily to the TSA multiple-choice questions while others may be more relevant to the TSA Writing Task.

The fact that universities are now looking at setting aptitude tests (such as the TSA) that involve critical-thinking skills, reflects the recognition that critical thinking is now being promoted in education generally. There is now an AS-level course (offered by the OCR Examination Board) in critical thinking. The course has five major areas: identifying the elements of reasoning; evaluating reasoning; recognising and evaluating assumptions; clarifying expressions and ideas; presenting a reasoned case in a clear, logical and coherent way. The assessment for this AS-level is by examination; there is no course work element and the examination is of a similar format to the TSA, i.e. questions related to passages and essays.

In the commercial field, professional psychometric testing has for many years employed critical-reasoning tests for similar reasons, i.e. the need for organisations to recruit or promote the right people, with the right skills, etc. In today's economic climate competition for jobs and training is intense and all the applicants find themselves in a selection pool of similarly qualified people, presenting a problem, not only for the applicant, but also for those who have a limited number of training places or job vacancies to offer. This makes the selection process difficult – from both perspectives. The result has been that the psychometrics profession, which comprises mainly test developers and publishers, has grown into a multi-million pound industry. Test developers are usually psychologists who specialise in testing (psychometrists) and it is usually their remit to construct tests of aptitude such as verbal, numerical, spatial ability, etc., as well as tests of other characteristics, such as personality.

When making selection decisions – whether they are for training, higher education or for job appointments – the area of critical thinking/reasoning is deemed to be very important. This is largely because these skills are important in performing the roles themselves, particularly those in management. Graduate/managerial level aptitude tests of verbal reasoning, which are basically assessing the understanding of words, grammar, spelling, word relationships, etc. may provide an objective assessment of a candidate's verbal ability. However, these types of test are seen by some to lack face validity (that is, they do not appear to be job related) when used for graduate/managerial roles. People of this level often object to being given 'IQ tests' and prefer an assessment that appears to replicate, to some extent, the content of the job, i.e. critically evaluating reports. It is also believed by some that classic verbal reasoning tests do not provide an indication of an individual's ability to think critically, therefore psychometrists have developed what are generally called critical-reasoning tests, which are similar in format to the TSA and described in the following section.

13. Critical thinking: example questions

Cambridge Assessment makes use of seven different types of question in the Thinking Skills element of the TSA and an explanation of these is provided below.

1. Summarising the main conclusion

Example question
A professional football club is considering screening players to determine whether they have a genetic disposition to be the next David Beckham or Steven Gerrard. Research has

provided evidence that genetic experiments on mice and rats has identified enhanced physical performance and that it is likely this could translate to humans. Also a study in America compared versions of the ACTN3 gene among a number of athletes and found that elite performers were more likely to have particular combinations of this gene variant. It is claimed that people with one version of the ACTN3 gene would excel as sprinters whilst those with another version would be better at endurance events.

What is the main conclusion of this passage?

A   Professional footballers may be genetically screened to identify potential David Beckhams or Steven Gerrards.

B   Genetic screening could have a role to play in identifying athletic talent.

C   Enhanced physical performance equates to enhanced athletic skills.

D   Potential sprinters and endurance athletes will be easier to identify with genetic screening.

E   The ACTN3 gene can identify future athletic talent.

Example question: answer and rationale

This question requires you to identify the **main conclusion** that can be drawn from the passage. A **conclusion** is simply a statement that is logical, that is a proposition that is arrived at after consideration of the evidence, arguments or premises. You are looking for the **main conclusion** that will follow from or be supported by the passage itself. The highlighted statement and rationale is correct.

A   Professional footballers may be genetically screened to identify potential David Beckhams or Steven Gerrards.

This is an incorrect answer as it picks up on the first part of the passage and does not take account of the other issues and evidence raised.

B   Genetic screening could have a role to play in identifying athletic talent.

This is the correct answer as the passage relates to two pieces of research, both of which are concerned with genetic disposition providing evidence of an individual's level of athletic performance, to identify better performers. These are only research studies and therefore the **main conclusion** following from and supported by the passage is that genetic screening *could* have a role to play in identifying athletic talent.

C   Enhanced physical performance equates to enhanced athletic skills.

This is an incorrect answer as it cannot be concluded from the content of the passage. Although it is being suggested that enhanced physical performance can equate to enhanced athletic skills this may only be the case where combinations of the ACTN3 gene variant exist. Other variants may still enhance physical performance but not necessarily enhance athleticism.

D   Potential sprinters and endurance athletes will be easier to identify with genetic screening.

This is an incorrect answer as although this may be what the passage is suggesting and could be used as the main conclusion it is not the best answer available. The answer only reflects part of the content of the passage and is not as comprehensive a conclusion as that contained in the correct answer.

E   The ACTN3 gene can identify future athletic talent.

This is an incorrect answer as it is almost stating conclusively that the ACTN3 gene can identify future athletic talent whereas the passage relates to two research studies: the first only being used on mice and rats; the second stating that 'elite performers were *more likely* to have particular combinations of this gene variant'. It is therefore *likely* that people without the gene variant may be elite performers.

2. Drawing a conclusion

Example question
The Department for Education plans to include eighteen social targets in Ofsted reports. It is suggested that schools would become broadly responsible for their pupils' safety, enjoyment and happiness. The social targets would require schools to keep records of matters such as drug problems, teenage pregnancy rates, criminal records, obesity levels, bullying, etc. The findings would be published in Ofsted's annual report which is widely used by parents to find out more about their child's school or when selecting a school in their area. The targets would also help to highlight differences between primary and secondary schools in similar circumstances.

Which one of the following conclusions is best supported by the passage?

A   Plans to give parents a true picture of children's lives.

B   Schools to be responsible for the safety, enjoyment and happiness of children.

C   Social issues in schools will be easier to identify.

D   Schools will be accountable for solving social problems.

E   Plans will reduce teenage pregnancy rates and drug use.

Example question: answer and rationale
A **conclusion** is simply a statement that is logical, that is a proposition arrived at after consideration of the evidence, arguments or premises. This requires you to examine each of

the statements and determine which one best provides a conclusion of the passage. The highlighted statement and rationale is correct.

> **A**   Plans to give parents a true picture of children's lives.
>
> This is the correct answer as it provides the one best conclusion of the passage. It is stated in the passage that the report 'is widely used by parents to find out more about their child's school or when selecting a school in their area.'

B   Schools to be responsible for the safety, enjoyment and happiness of children.

This is an incorrect answer as the passage states that 'schools would become broadly responsible' as opposed to the statement itself that suggests total responsibility.

C   Social issues in schools will be easier to identify.

This is an incorrect answer as nowhere in the passage does it suggest that it will be easier to identify social issues as this may be determined by the willingness or otherwise of pupils to provide the information required by the targets.

D   Schools will be accountable for solving social problems.

This is an incorrect answer, as even though it is suggested that schools may collect information identifying the social problems of their pupils, it cannot be concluded that the schools will be accountable for these problems.

E   Plans will reduce teenage pregnancy rates and drug use.

This is an incorrect answer, as even though schools may identify the incidence of teenage pregnancies and drug use, the plans are not designed to reduce these, although this could conceivably be a by-product.

3. Identifying an assumption

Example question

The demand for octopus meat is becoming widespread across the retail food industry and conservationists are concerned many species of octopus could be extinct within 10 years. The calls from conservationists for octopus meat to be taken off the menu in restaurants and gastro pubs, and a boycott by high street stores, are being ignored. The promotion of octopus meat dishes by celebrity chefs is also flying in the face of conservation. It is believed that 30% of octopus meat caught within European waters is exported to Far East markets.

Which one of the following statements can be assumed from the passage?

A   Octopus are only hunted for their meat.

B   Celebrity chefs are not concerned with conservation.

C   A ban on octopus meat in restaurants would protect some species.

D   The Far East is the biggest consumer of octopus meat.

E   Consumer demand is directly related to advertising.

Example question: answer and rationale

An **assumption** is a proposition that is taken for granted, that is, as if it were known to be true. It is a statement that can be surmised or postulated given the overall context of the passage. This question is asking you to identify which statement can be surmised or postulated from the passage. In identifying an **assumption** the correct statement will not actually be stated in the passage so it is for you to determine the main argument and look for the reasoning to support this conclusion. You need to read the passage carefully to identify the overall argument and determine which one option best answers the question posed. The highlighted statement and rationale is correct.

A   Octopus are only hunted for their meat.

This is an incorrect answer as the passage only deals with octopus in relation to their meat for human consumption whereas the meat or other parts of the octopus may be used for other purposes.

B   Celebrity chefs are not concerned with conservation.

This is an incorrect answer as although the passage states, 'The promotion of octopus meat dishes by celebrity chefs . . .', it does not follow that such chefs are unconcerned about the conservation of octopuses.

C   A ban on octopus meat in restaurants would protect some species.

This is an incorrect answer as it cannot be determined whether or not a ban on octopus meat would protect some species.

D   The Far East is the biggest consumer of octopus meat.

This is an incorrect answer as although the passage states that, '30% of octopus meat caught within European waters is exported to Far East markets', there is no information about the export of octopus meat caught in non-European waters.

E   Consumer demand is directly related to advertising.

This is the correct answer as although the word 'advertising' is not used in the passage it can be assumed from a number of the statements. Octopus meat is advertised by being on the menu in restaurants and gastro pubs, being on sale in high street stores and included in recipes by celebrity chefs.

4. Assessing the impact of additional evidence

Example question

There are about 2 million grey squirrels in the UK, compared to 150,000 red squirrels, the majority of which are in Scotland. Black squirrels, a genetic mutation of the grey squirrel, are also expanding rapidly and there are already about 25,000 in the eastern counties of England alone. The black squirrel was first spotted in the early part of the 20th Century, and they are known to be more aggressive than their grey and red counterparts. What this indicates is that the black squirrel population may well overtake that of the red squirrels and eventually that of the grey squirrels.

Which one of the following statements, if true, would most weaken the above argument?

A   Farmers have no hesitation in shooting squirrels, considering them to be a pest.

B   The population of squirrels generally has increased due to householders feeding them.

C   English Nature has undertaken several initiatives to increase the number of red squirrels in England.

D   Research in the USA has found that squirrel mutations peak and decrease after 100 years.

E   The Woodland Trust disputes the published figures.

Example question: answer and rationale

In assessing the impact of additional evidence you are looking for which statement would *weaken* the argument of the passage. So you first need to determine what the argument is and then consider the effect of each statement on the conclusion. The highlighted statement and rationale is correct.

A   Farmers have no hesitation in shooting squirrels, considering them to be a pest.

This is an incorrect answer as it does not *weaken* or impact on the argument contained within the passage.

B   The population of squirrels generally has increased due to householders feeding them.

This is an incorrect answer as it does not *weaken* or impact on the argument contained within the passage.

C   English Nature has undertaken several initiatives to increase the number of red squirrels in England.

This is an incorrect answer as it does not *weaken* or impact on the argument contained within the passage.

> **D**   Research in the USA has found that squirrel mutations peak and decrease after 100 years.

This is the correct answer as the passage, apart from providing certain figures in relation to the population of grey, red and black squirrels, also states that the black squirrel population is increasing considerably due in part to its aggressive behaviour. This answer suggests that as the black squirrel is a mutation of the grey squirrel its population will peak within the next few years and then decrease. This is contrary to the thrust of the passage of an increasing black squirrel population.

E   The Woodland Trust disputes the published figures.

This is an incorrect answer as it does not *weaken* or impact on the argument contained within the passage.

5. Detecting reasoning errors

Example question

In 1953 the European Convention for the Protection of Human Rights and Fundamental Freedoms gave full legal protection, for those countries making up the Council of Europe, to the most fundamental rights and freedoms necessary in democratic societies. The Convention was drawn up when countries were coming to terms with the total disregard from human rights and freedoms in the wake of the Second World War. Since being adopted by the majority of countries throughout Europe, the Convention is now part of international law and individuals can seek help from the European Court of Human Rights where their civil liberties have been violated by the state. However, few practical remedies are available even where an applicant is successful.

Which one of the following statements contains a flaw in its argument?

A   The European Convention applies to most of Europe.

B   The Convention was implemented over half a century ago.

C   War breaches human rights.

D   Violations of human rights cannot always be remedied through the Court.

E   Freedom is a democratic right.

Sample question: answer and rationale

Reasoning is the mental (cognitive) process of looking for reasons for beliefs, conclusions, actions or feelings. The questions will normally ask you to determine the **flaw** in an argument so you are looking for which statement does not follow from reasons given for the conclusion. The highlighted statement and rationale is correct.

A   The European Convention applies to most of Europe.

This is an incorrect answer as it is directly stated in the passage that the Convention has been 'adopted by the majority of countries throughout Europe'.

B   The Convention was implemented over half a century ago.

This is an incorrect answer as it is directly stated in the passage that, 'In 1953 the European Convention for the Protection of Human Rights and Fundamental Freedoms gave full legal protection . . .'.

C   War breaches human rights.

This is the correct answer as it cannot be inferred from the information in the passage. It could be made as an assertion generally, given the reference to some of the breaches made in the wake of the Second World War, but there is no evidence in the passage to support this general claim.

D   Violations of human rights cannot always be remedied through the Court.

This is an incorrect answer as it is directly stated in the passage that, 'However, few practical remedies are available even where an applicant is successful'.

E   Freedom is a democratic right.

This is an incorrect answer as it is directly stated in the passage, 'fundamental rights and freedoms necessary in democratic societies'.

6. Matching argument

Example question

Peter seems to have lost a lot of weight over the last 3 months. He must have found a good diet or cut down on his alcohol consumption. I know he is still a heavy drinker so it must be his new diet.

Which one of the following most closely parallels the reasoning used in the above argument?

A   Anyone who smokes cigarettes must be unhealthy. Lillian smokes at least 20 cigarettes a day so she must be pretty unfit.

B   I sent an urgent email to a colleague at another branch but she has not responded. I know she's been working in Holland so she must still be away. She always responds promptly to emails.

C   Giving up smoking is very difficult when you first stop but after 2 months the craving for nicotine eases. Brian stopped smoking 6 weeks ago so the craving for nicotine is getting less and less.

D Laura wants to keep slim and healthy and knows she must be careful what she eats and drinks. Because she wants to keep slim and healthy she eats carefully and does not drink alcohol.

E Kul runs 5 kilometres every weekday and 10 kilometres on Saturday mornings. People who regularly exercise should be fit and healthy. Kul should be fit and healthy.

Example question: answer and rationale

In a **matching argument** type question you are looking for a similarity in the structure or pattern of the argument that is reproduced in the correct statement.

In relation to the passage above, we can look for a structure to see if statements have been repeated and which could be represented with the letters X or Y. Note that such statements may not be exactly the same. Two such statements that are contained in the passage are: 'Peter is on a good diet', represented by X, and 'Peter has cut down on his alcohol consumption', represented by Y. Either X is true or Y is true. Y cannot be true, so X must be true. The highlighted statement and rationale is correct.

A Anyone who smokes cigarettes must be unhealthy. Lillian smokes at least 20 cigarettes a day so she must be pretty unfit.

This is an incorrect answer as the passage has a different structure. All people who do X are Y, i.e. Lillian does X (smokes cigarettes) and therefore Lillian is Y (unhealthy).

B I sent an urgent email to a colleague at another branch but she has not responded. I know she's been working in Holland so she must still be away. She always responds promptly to emails.

This is the correct answer as the passage has the same structure. Two statements that are repeated in a slightly different way in the passage are: 'my colleague must be away', represented by X, and 'she always responds promptly to email', represented by Y. Either X is true or Y is true. Y cannot be true, so X must be true.

C Giving up smoking is very difficult when you first stop but after 2 months the craving for nicotine eases. Brian stopped smoking 6 weeks ago so the craving for nicotine is getting less and less.

This is an incorrect answer as the passage has a different structure. Most people who do X succeed in Y, i.e. Brian has done X (stopped smoking for 6 weeks) and will succeed in Y (craving for nicotine is getting less and less).

D Laura wants to keep slim and healthy and knows she must be careful what she eats and drinks. Because she wants to keep slim and healthy she eats carefully and does not drink alcohol.

This is an incorrect answer as the passage has a different structure. If Laura wants X, she has to do Y, i.e. if Laura wants X (to keep slim and healthy), she has to do Y (eat carefully and drink no alcohol).

E Kul runs 5 kilometres every weekday and 10 kilometres on Saturday mornings. People who regularly exercise should usually be fit and healthy. Kul should be fit and healthy.

This is an incorrect answer as the passage has a different structure. People who do X are usually Y, i.e. Kul does X (regular exercise) and so he should be Y (fit and healthy).

7. Applying principles

Example question
People who participate in high risk sporting activities such as mountaineering or rock climbing know the possible consequences of their sport and should be required to have insurance to indemnify them against the costs incurred when an accident occurs. This indemnity can be used to cover the considerable cost to the emergency services, such as mountain rescue teams and RAF rescue helicopters. Those not insured should be sued for the retrieval of the costs.

Which one of the following best illustrates the principle underlying the argument in the passage?

A People who have accidents in speedboats should be asked to make a voluntary contribution where they use the services of the Royal National Lifeboat Institute (RNLI).

B Health treatment, whether arising from everyday life activities or from some form of addiction, should be provided without cost to any individual.

C People who do not pay income tax or national insurance should not benefit from state subsidies.

D Private medical insurance is the antithesis of the NHS, undermining a fair and equitable health service for the benefit of all.

E Road tax and insurance should equally apply to cyclists as it does to drivers of motorised vehicles.

Sample question: answer and rationale
Generally, **principle** means a standard or rule of personal conduct or a set of such moral rules. The passage will contain a particular principle usually in the form of a general recommendation and this will be reproduced in the correct statement.

The conclusion from the above passage is that people who participate in high risk sporting activities should have insurance to indemnify them in relation to any costs incurred when use is made of emergency services. This reasoning relies on the principle that if you take part in high risk activities you should pay for the services required in an emergency. The highlighted statement and rationale is correct.

A   People who have accidents in speedboats should be asked to make a voluntary contribution where they use the services of the Royal National Lifeboat Institute (RNLI).

This is an incorrect answer as it does not suggest that people in speedboats have insurance indemnity to cover the costs incurred by the RNLI.

B   Health treatment, whether arising from everyday life activities or from some form of addiction, should be provided without cost to any individual.

This is an incorrect answer as it does not apply to the principle of the main passage but recommends health treatment is free irrespective of a person's lifestyle.

C   People who do not pay income tax or national insurance should not benefit from state subsidies.

This is an incorrect answer as it does not apply to the principle of the main passage but recommends no state benefits for those who do not contribute tax or national insurance.

D   Private medical insurance is the antithesis of the NHS, undermining a fair and equitable health service for the benefit of all.

This is an incorrect answer as it does not apply to the principle of the main passage but suggests that private medical insurance is basically inequitable.

E   Road tax and insurance should equally apply to cyclists as it does to drivers of motorised vehicles.

This is the correct answer as it applies the principle to cyclists as it does to those taking part in high risk sporting activities, i.e. insurance indemnity in the event of accidents.

Chapter 4

Thinking Skills Assessment practice test

14. Introduction

You will be presented with a question paper, either pencil/paper or online, and will be allowed 90 minutes to complete the test. There are a total of 50 questions, 25 problem solving and 25 critical thinking, and these two types of question will be mixed throughout the paper.

When you get the question paper read the instructions carefully to refresh your memory of what is required.

In the assessment itself you are not permitted to use a calculator but may use a dictionary (book or electronic). Any rough working would be done either in the test booklet or, if online, on the area indicated in the instructions.

The following practice questions replicate those used in the Thinking Skills Assessment, but it is a decision for you to make whether you time constrain their completion to the 90 minutes.

Before completing this section it might be useful to refresh your memory as to the two suggested strategies often used in answering these types of questions. The strategies can be found on pages 11 and 12. Try using both strategies for different questions and see which one suits you better.

The assessment is not a test of knowledge but of fundamental intellectual skills. Do not use your own knowledge of a particular issue when answering any of the questions.

Remember each question has a possible choice of five answers and only ONE answer is correct.

The correct answer to each of the questions is produced at the end of the section. The next section then examines the rationale for both the correct and incorrect answers.

There is also a demonstration test available on the Cambridge Assessment website which you might consider completing after undertaking the practice test and checking the answers and rationale for each question.

15. Thinking Skills Assessment: practice test

1   A study of boys and girls aged 12 to 15 years indicated those who regularly read comics were more creative in their writing and were much better communicators compared with those who did not read comics.

From the indicated findings of this study it can be implied that:

A   the communication skills of children can be affected by reading.

B   children who read comics are better at public speaking.

C   children who read books are likely to be more creative compared to those who don't read books.

D   a child's communication skills are influenced by the type of comic they read.

E   it is generally accepted that girls are better communicators than boys in their teenage years.

2   A very successful scientific research company has appointed a design and marketing agency to come up with a new name for their company. They want a name that relates strongly to their professional ethos and business area. In addition, they want a name that can be displayed in their office and vehicle windows that will read the same vertically when viewed from inside or outside.

Which of the following names would suit their requirement?

A   MAXIM

B   MATRIX

C   AXIOM

D   WHICH

E   ATOM

3   J & B Engineering Limited undertook a validation study in order to determine the relationship between their recruitment tests and job performance (JP). The approximate overlaps of the tests with JP are as follows: numerical (N) 50%; verbal (V) 20%; Abstract (A) 33%. V and N also overlap with each other by 15% and V and N overlap with A by 33%.

Which one of the following Venn diagrams depicts this information?

A

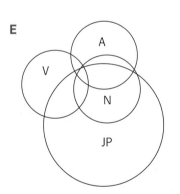

N

V

JP

A

B

N

V

A

JP

C

V

N

A

JP

D

A

V

N

JP

E

A

V

N

JP

4   We all have to pay for a television licence (barring concessions) even if we never watch the BBC and only watch the commercial channels. You could use your TV just to watch DVDs or videos; or you could just watch ITV or Satellite channels but you will still have to pay the same as someone who only watches the BBC. This system is not equitable and should be changed.

Which one of the following statements is based on a similar principle to the TV licence argument?

A   People with high incomes should not receive child benefit.

B   Frequent travellers using bus, train or plane should pay less than occasional travellers.

C   People who earn more should subsidise those who earn less so that they can afford private health care.

D   Road tax is unfair for someone who has low mileage and we should be charged road tax on mileage bandings.

E   Free bus passes should be means tested.

5   Magic Books Ltd publishes a range of children's books. Their books range from short to long text and they always have an illustration on the centre fold. The books range in size from 16 pages upwards but they are always in multiples of 16 pages, e.g. 16, 32, 48, 64 . . . Page one of the book is always the front cover.

The illustration on the centre fold could have which one of the following page numbering?

A   23 and 24

B   64 and 65

C   14 and 15

D   63 and 64

E   78 and 79

6   The number of first class honours degrees awarded at Oxford and Cambridge in English related subjects is more than twice the number of any other UK university even though the degree requirements are almost identical. However, research indicates a clear parity with Oxford and Cambridge in entrance qualifications with over 30% of other universities.

Which one of the following is an underlying assumption of the above argument?

A   Entrance qualifications are a poor predictor of future attainment.

B   Degree results are prone to fluctuation.

C   English degrees are easier at Oxford and Cambridge.

D   Oxford and Cambridge attract students with higher potential.

E   Oxford and Cambridge attract the best lecturers.

7   EnergyHeat and Warmhomes provide electricity on the following basis: EnergyHeat has a standing charge of £30 per quarter and charges 15p per kWh; Warmhomes has a standing charge of £24 per quarter and charges 20p per kWh.

How many kWh would you have to use in 1 month for the cost to be the same with both companies, calculating the standing charge pro rata?

A   30 kWh

B   40 kWh

C   50 kWh

D   60 kWh

E   70 kWh

8   The government is considering forcing single parents of children as young as two to seek work despite fears such moves could push more into poverty during the recession. Savings in benefits under the shake-up would be used to help fund universal childcare and higher maternity leave payments. The policy is one of a raft of radical steps being urged by a political party think-tank.

Which one of the following statements can be implied from the passage?

A   The think-tank's deliberations do not consider the current economic climate.

B   Single parents forced into employment would benefit from higher childcare payments.

C   Single mothers who were forced to find work would be better off.

D   Benefit payments could be withdrawn from those refusing to seek work.

E   Higher maternity leave payments would benefit single mothers following their child's birth.

9   The gemstone table below details the hardness, refractive index, and relative density of various gems.

GEMSTONE	HARDNESS	REFRACTIVE INDEX	RELATIVE DENSITY
Alexandrite	8.5	1.746–1.763	3.70–3.78
Amber	2.5	1.539–1.545	1.05–1.09
Citrine	7.0	1.544–1.533	2.65
Emerald	8.0	1.565–1.602	2.67–2.78
Diamond	10.0	2.417–2.419	3.50–3.53
Ruby	9.0	1.762–1.778	3.97–4.05
Sapphire	9.0	1.762–1.788	3.95–4.03
Tanzanite	7.0	1.691–1.700	3.35
Topaz	8.0	1.609–1.643	3.49–3.57
Zircon	7.5	1.810–2.024	3.93–4.73

What are the mean value of hardness and the mode value of relative density (using the highest value from the range where necessary)?

A   7.65 and 3.57

B   7.65 and 3.55

C   7.75 and 3.55

D   7.65 and 3.53

E   7.5 and 3.55

10   The aeroplane has opened up worldwide travel possibilities to millions of people. It used to be the mode of transport of the jet-setting rich but the availability of cut-price flights has made flying a relatively cheap option for all. The level of pollution from aircraft has also naturally risen and individuals who fly regularly significantly increase their 'carbon footprint'. Air travel is now a major contributor to global warming and must be regulated to prevent further damage to the worldwide climate. To ignore the warnings will be detrimental to the survival of Earth as we know it.

Which one of the following statements best summarises the main conclusion of the above argument?

A   The world is likely to end due to air travel.

B   A ban on planes would reduce pollution.

C   The problem of aircraft emissions and the number of flights needs to be resolved.

D   Aircraft flights cause changes to the world climate.

E   Cut-price flights and the increasing number of airlines are to blame for global warming.

11   A farmer owns land that totals 254 acres. His house and personal garden take up 1.75 acres, barns and other farm buildings take up 2.25 acres. The remaining land is split between 60% pasture land and 40% arable. The farmer always rests a quarter of his arable land each year, 4% is taken up by tracks and hedges and 1% fails to yield any crops.

What is the acreage of productive arable land in a year?

A   100 acres

B   105 acres

C   30 acres

D   75 acres

E   70 acres

12 During a general election all British citizens aged 18 and over are eligible to vote. The choice of candidate, political party and the strength of the campaign will influence the voter. However, they do have the choice of whether or not to vote. The candidate with the most votes in each constituency will win that seat. The political party with the majority of seats will form the next government. Therefore, the new party will have the support of the majority of the eligible voting public.

Which one of the following statements best identifies the flaw in the above argument?

A   Campaigners can influence the voting patterns of the British public.

B   Elected candidates could resign whichever way the vote goes.

C   A high percentage of the public do not vote and we can never be sure what impact their votes would have on the result.

D   The system of voting in Britain is unfair and we should change to a system of proportional representation.

E   Voters can change their minds regularly and therefore results are not pre-dictable.

13 We have oil-fired central heating in our home and home office that we keep on during the months of October to March. We are allowed to allocate 20% of the bill as a business expense. Our oil tank has an electronic meter that shows the total litres used and we record this on the 1st of each month.

	LITRES USED
1 October	1058
1 November	1217
1 December	1399
1 January	1596
1 February	1815
1 March	2032

During which month did the home office use most oil?

A   October

B   February

C   March

D   January

E   December

14 If Top Ten Ltd does not increase its dividends then attracting new investors will be difficult and this will affect business expansion plans. This, in turn, would restrict the growth of the business and in real terms could result in a decline of the market share. Either shareholders should be better rewarded or the company must shelve its expansion plans.

Which one of the following statements best expresses the conclusion of this argument?

A Attracting new investors in business is difficult.

B If dividends are not increased the business may not grow.

C Shareholders will have to accept small dividends.

D Top Ten Ltd may close due to a lack of expansion.

E If dividends are increased the business will have more shareholders.

15 The table below shows the number of males and females from a study of 100 people that purchase various types of insurance.

Male	Type of Insurance	Female
54	Car	36
44	Home	45
37	Contents	45
22	Health	17
9	Employment Protection	5
5	Travel	5
7	Sport	2
14	Pet	15
14	Dental	15
3	Business Liability	1

The average difference between the number of men and women that purchase Home, Sport and Dental insurance is?

A 3

B 2

C 5

D −1

E 1

16 The level of subscription paid by individuals for private health care does not relate to their level of health. Some individuals pay several times more than others and some pay less but their life expectancies are not significantly different. The suggestion that you receive what you pay for is therefore irrelevant in terms of private health care.

Which one of the following statements is an underlying assumption of the above argument?

A   The cost of private health care is not a measure of its effectiveness.

B   The more you pay the better the health provision.

C   Private health care is no better than the National Health Service.

D   Individuals should be prepared to pay for health care.

E   Life expectancy is a reliable measure of the efficacy of private health care.

17 What is the volume of the following cuboid in cm^3 ?

A   187500 cm^3

B   18750 cm^3

C   187.5 cm^3

D   18.75 cm^3

E   1875 cm^3

18 There are many mysterious facts about the number 23 and the number 41.

Twenty-three is the lowest prime number with two digits; it has been the subject of two films; Darwin's *Origin of Species* was published in 1859 (digits add to 23); in the movie *Airport* the bomber sits in seat 23; the digits of the 9/11/2001 attacks add to 23; Michael Jordan and David Beckham have worn number 23 shirts; each parent contributes 23 chromosomes to a child; the Knights Templar had 23 Grand Masters; these are just a few of the facts. Forty-one is the 23rd smallest prime number; it is the atomic number of niobium; it is the number of the last symphony of Mozart; it is a song by the Dave Matthews Band; it represents the 39 lashes Jesus Christ received plus one for the spear in his side and one for the crown of thorns; Charlton Heston's slave number in Ben-Hur was 41; George H W Bush was the 41st President of the USA; 35 mm colour negative film is developed using the C-41 process; again, these are just a few of the facts. Therefore, these numbers are more than numbers that come between 22 and 24 and 40 and 42.

Which one of the following is the best statement of the flaw in the passage above?

A   Any number could be related to a series of facts.

B   The use of these numbers has been chosen in some cases and could be coincidental in others.

C   David Beckham has not always worn a number twenty-three shirt as he used to wear a number seven shirt.

D   The links between some facts and the numbers are very tenuous.

E   Twenty-three and forty-one are not prime numbers.

19   After dropping off their children at the local playgroup four mothers were discussing how many dolls each of their daughters had. The four daughters were aged 1, 2, 3 and 4 and they had one, two, three and four dolls but not necessarily respectively. Elizabeth has more dolls than her age. Sarah is older than Alisha. Only one girl has the same number of dolls as her age. Mia has fewer dolls than Sarah and the girl aged 3 has two dolls. Mia is the youngest.

How old is Alisha and how many dolls does she have?

A   Alisha is 1 year old and she has four dolls.

B   Alisha is 2 years old and she has two dolls.

C   Alisha is 3 years old and she has two dolls.

D   Alisha is 3 years old and she has three dolls.

E   Alisha is 4 years old and she has one doll.

20   For a documentary on 'The Knife Culture' a survey revealed that up to 5% of the population believe they will become victims of knife crime during the next year; the actual statistic is 0.01%. The fear of 'The Knife Culture' is more predominant with adults even though the group most affected is young males. The internet has been the main media used to access information about knives and knife crime. Whilst some of these sites are developed for valid reasons, some appear to glorify knife crime making it more fearful than it really is. It is time these sites were removed from the internet.

Which one of the following statements, if factual, would reduce the power of the above argument?

A The internet is too graphic in its portrayal of knife crime.

B Most people are unaware of the statistics of knife crime.

C Knife crime has replaced other forms of violent crime.

D Adults are less likely to access internet sites detailing knife crime.

E Surveys have accurately identified the population's views on knife crime.

21 Mum and Dad are taking their children to the cinema. Mum is taking the youngest child to see *Beauty and the Beast*, Dad is going to watch *Rocky V*, their teenage daughter is meeting her friends to watch *High School Musical*, and their twin boys are watching a cartoon hour followed by a game of ten-pin bowling. The Majestic Cinema and Bowling Alley listings are below.

The Majestic Cinema and Bowling Alley	
Ten-pin bowling	Hourly at a quarter to the hour Commencing 09.45 to 20.45 Duration 90 minutes
Rocky V	3 hourly at a quarter past the hour Commencing 16.15 to 19.15 Duration 2 hours 45 minutes
High School Musical	3 hourly at 20 past the hour Commencing 13.20 to 19.20 Duration 2 hours 15 minutes
Beauty and the Beast	3 hourly at a quarter to the hour Commencing 12.45 to 18.45 Duration 2 hours 5 minutes
Cartoon hour	On the hour Commencing 11.00 to 20.00

Mum and Dad are taking the whole family for a pizza afterwards. Mum and Dad want to begin watching the films as early as possible. What time do they need to arrive at the cinema, including 15 minutes to purchase tickets and drinks etc., and what is the earliest possible time they can meet in the foyer afterwards?

A 15.30 and 19.00

B 15.45 and 18.15

C 15.45 and 19.15

D 15.30 and 19.15

E 15.45 and 19.00

22 In 1948 the London Olympics cost £761,688 and made a profit of £29,420. The projected cost for the London Olympics was originally £2.4bn but this has now risen to £9.35bn. The Olympic ideal is about the brotherhood of man but it now seems to be about each country outshining previous holders of the event in the splendour of its show. This spurious form of national glory is defended by the palliative promises of a significant long-term economic boost for London's East End but it is believed these will fall far short of expectations.

What main conclusion can be drawn from this passage?

A The Olympic ideal has been lost at the expense of consumerism.

B The Olympic Games in London is seeking to provide bigger and better venues than the previous Games in China.

C Urban regeneration and other benefits may be the legacy of the Olympic Games in London's East End.

D There has been a fivefold increase in the projected costs for hosting the Olympic Games in London compared to the original figure.

E Part of the £9.35bn, the projected cost of hosting the Olympic Games, will be met by a post-Games economic boost.

23 The diagram below shows a round serviette which has three identical segments torn out from around the edge.

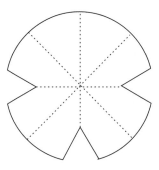

The dotted lines represent the folds of the serviette. Which one of the following diagrams would not be possible once folded along any one of the folds?

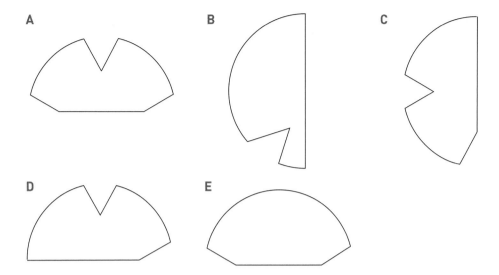

24 The increase of food centres selling products that are produced locally reduces the cost to the environment and boosts the local economy. It would be preferable to encourage the growth of this business in favour of building more and more supermarkets. Encouraging the public to shop at these centres would reduce the level of wasted packaging, not to mention the wasted transport costs, etc. The land earmarked for future supermarkets could be used to build more local food centres with small food production units which would be more beneficial to everyone.

Which one of the following statements best depicts the main conclusion of the above argument?

A   Food centres reduce the levels of waste.

B   Land can be used for local food businesses.

C   Locally produced food reduces the need for mass produced food.

D   Local food centres are preferable to supermarkets.

E   Small local food centres do not use as many resources as supermarkets.

25 The following table shows the percentage fall in house value prices during the past 12 months as a result of the worldwide economic recession.

Percentage fall in world house prices	
Slovakia	-31%
Russia	-26%
Hong Kong	-18%
US	-15%
UK	-10%
Ireland	-8%
China	-5%
Germany	-3%
France	-2%
Spain	-2%

According to this table which of the following is true?

A The average percentage fall in house prices in EEC (Slovakia, UK, Ireland, Germany, France and Spain) is less than half that of the non-EEC countries shown.

B The percentage fall in the price of a house in the US is almost half that of Slovakia and more than twice that of Ireland.

C The average price of a house in Ireland has fallen less than the UK but more than China.

D The combined percentage fall of the bottom five countries in the table is less than the percentage fall in Russia alone.

E The combined percentage fall of the US, China and France is equal to that of Russia.

26 As with all drugs the side effects of taking antidepressants can be mild with some and extreme with others. The evidence to support one antidepressant drug over another is non-existent, therefore the choice is often made on the basis of the known side effects. The extensive use of SSRIs has come about mainly because they are considered safer than more toxic drugs in terms of overdosing. The press have published disturbing links between suicide and violent behaviour and the use of SSRIs. It has also been claimed that these drugs have great risks when used with other drugs and can have differing side effects with young people. There is a lack of full understanding about how antidepressants and depression affect the brain. Even the drug companies admit to a lack of understanding about how their drugs work.

Which one of the following conclusions can be drawn from the above passage?

A SSRIs are safer as a common form of suicide was to overdose on toxic anti-depressants.

B Using alternative medicine such as St John's Wort is preferable to SSRIs.

C More extensive research needs to be undertaken by all concerned to extend the understanding of how antidepressants and depression affect the brain.

D The drugs used to treat depression are no better than placebos and should not be prescribed as freely as they are.

E The use of 'talking therapies' to treat depression would be more effective and safer than conventional drugs such as SSRIs.

27 The following table shows two sets of results for a range of aptitude tests taken by a group of males and females over a period of one year (all the tests are the raw scores out of 100).

	Males 1st result	Females 1st result	Males 2nd result	Females 2nd result
Verbal	76	80	78	82
Numerical	80	78	81	81
Abstract	65	66	67	67
Mechanical	77	61	78	62
Spatial	71	69	72	70
Checking	68	77	69	78

In relation to the two sets of results which ONE of the following options is correct?

(NB: the ratios shown have been rounded to the nearest whole number)

A *Mechanical aptitude test* – ratio of 3.5:4 males to females
Checking aptitude test – ratio of 4:3 males to females
4:3 is the largest ratio difference

B *Mechanical aptitude test* – ratio of 4:3 males to females
Checking aptitude test – ratio of 3.5:4 males to females
4:3 is the largest ratio difference

C *Mechanical aptitude test* – ratio of 8:6 males to females
Checking aptitude test – ratio of 7:8 males to females
7:8 is the largest ratio difference

D   *Mechanical aptitude test* – ratio of 4:3 males to females
Checking aptitude test – ratio of 3:5 males to females
The ratio difference is the same

E   *Mechanical aptitude test* – ratio of 3.5:3 males to females
Checking aptitude test – ratio of 3:3.5 males to females
3.5:3 is the largest ratio difference

28   Extract from a government green paper on universities:

There are questions about the answerability of universities when there are complaints from students, staff or the public. At present complaints, whether of academic inadequacy or neglect, financial extravagance, unfair treatment in examinations, or political bias in teaching, cannot effectively be pursued by the vice-chancellor, or in some cases the visitor. But universities, though dependent on public funds, are privileged institutions with a very significant degree of self-government. It is important that they should take complaints seriously and be seen to do so. The Government is concerned about the present apparent lack of accountability and is discussing with the Committee of Vice-Chancellors and Principals what might be done.

Which of the sentences in the paper is a statement of principle?

A   'There are questions about the answerability of universities when there are complaints . . .'

B   '. . . complaints . . . of academic inadequacy or neglect . . . cannot effectively be pursued by the vice-chancellor . . .'

C   'But universities, though dependent on public funds, are privileged institutions with a very significant degree of self-government.'

D   '. . . they should take complaints seriously and be seen to do so.'

E   'The Government is concerned about the present apparent lack of account-ability . . .'

29 The following table details the carriage charges in pounds and pence for some of
the services provided by Ontrack Couriers for UK mainland deliveries.

ITEM	WEIGHT	SAME DAY	NEXT DAY	3 DAYS	1 WEEK
Letter	0–100 g	1.00	0.75	–	–
Package	0–1 kg	9.95	6.95	5.95	3.95
	Up to 5 kg	11.95	8.95	7.95	5.95
	Up to 10 kg	13.95	11.95	9.95	7.95
	Up to 25 kg	15.95	13.95	11.95	9.95
	Up to 50 kg	21.99	19.99	17.99	15.95
	Up to 100 kg	47.99	40.99	33.95	30.99

A business that receives a special rate which is discounted by 20%, on packages
only, wishes to send the following: 50 letters same day, 100 letters next day, 10
packages weighing 4 kg each 3-day delivery, 15 packages weighing 19 kg each
same day, 3 packages weighing 49 kg 1-week delivery and 2 packages weighing
83 kg 3-day delivery.

What will be the total cost?

A   £492.00

B   £144.40

C   £347.60

D   £448.55

E   £472.60

30 Our insurance company is looking to recruit a sales director who has the confidence to attend conferences where he/she will be required to make promotional
presentations. We have short-listed to three applicants but the applicant with the
best sales management record has not come out too well on the personality test
that we use as an integral part of our recruitment process. The personality test
indicates that he is not very socially bold and that he will probably exert a great
deal of nervous energy when placed at the centre of attention. It also suggests that
he would not be comfortable in large social gatherings. We have, after
consideration, decided not to offer him the post.

Which one of the following statements best highlights the flaw in this argument?

A   The assumption is made that he has no coping strategies for such situations.

B   The assumption is that introverts cannot succeed in sales.

C   Other factors from the recruitment process are not considered.

D It assumes that the personality test is predictive of behaviour.

E It assumes that sales directors need to be socially bold.

31 Getaway airport is surrounded by several tall radio masts with warning lights. The lights on the highest masts flash red every 2½ minutes, the medium masts flash blue every 4½ minutes and the lowest masts flash orange every 6 minutes. Periodically they all flash at the same time.

What is the shortest length of the interval between synchronised flashes?

A 90 minutes

B 13 minutes

C 180 minutes

D 30 minutes

E 10 minutes

32 Gordon understands that to become a successful writer he needs to apply his writing skills and that he also needs to put in a considerable amount of work. He also needs to work hard on producing a book that will capture the imagination of the book-buying public. Gordon is determined to write a best seller and he will be working hard to achieve this.

Which one of the following scenarios most closely parallels the reasoning of the above argument?

A Jennifer really wants to be a very successful actress and has dreams of winning an Oscar. She has just enrolled with RADA and will soon be on her way to her ambition.

B If you want to be very successful in finance you have to gain experience with large city firms. I do not wish to leave our small town and will have to lower my aims.

C The marriage guidance counsellor is hoping she will be able to reunite the estranged couple. They both really want this and she will talk to both of them at the next session.

D Steven really wants to achieve a first in his geology degree and has to work very hard on his assignments, projects and exam revision. He is confident that his hard work will pay dividends.

E Billy knows that to expand his building business he needs new skills such as plumbing. He has enrolled on an NVQ course in plumbing and will soon be installing bathrooms.

33 The table below shows the daily mileage for the Easy Travel Coach Company.

	Mon	Tue	Wed	Thu	Fri	Sat	Sun
Mileage	2,000	4,000	1,500	2,000	7,250	8,750	5,900

The MD of the company wants the IT office to plot the mileage on a bar chart. The IT office allocates the task to a new member of staff who forgets to insert the detail on each axis and also enters the mileage in a different order.

Which one of the following bar charts is representative of the data?

A

B

C

D

E
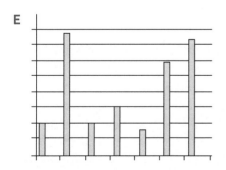

34 The government is considering ways of censoring the internet with the aim of protecting children. One way will be to have two blacklists: one blocking illegal material such as pornography, and one that blocks things deemed unsuitable for children – determined by a government agency. A recent poll showed 86% of the public were against internet censorship and civil liberties groups consider it an infringement of human rights. A previous trial with ISP content filtering technology had the effect of reducing internet speeds (up to 86%), blocking a large number of innocuous pages (up to 7.8%) and letting unsafe pages through (up to 13%).

Which one of the following is the best conclusion that can be drawn from the extract?

A Children will see their internet speeds downgraded.

B 14% of the public support central censorship for children.

C Prohibiting people access to child pornography is an infringement of their human rights.

D Censorship is legitimate to protect children from harm.

E Filtering technology can never block children accessing unsafe pages.

35 The park and ride bus runs Monday to Thursday from 7.30 am to 5.30 pm and from 8.30 am to 6.30 pm on Friday to Sunday. There is no break in this service and each journey lasts 8 minutes. Each bus waits 6 minutes for passengers and at very busy times the wait can be as little as 4 minutes.

In any one day what is the maximum possible number of bus journeys?

A 40

B 50

C 55

D 60

E 75

36 In the global warming debate governments are facing stiff targets on reducing carbon use which has seen the rush to low carbon fuels made from crops. The UK government introduced its Renewable Transport Fuels Obligation requiring that 2.5% of all petrol and diesel is to be made from biofuels, to be increased to 5.75% over two years. However, there is a downside. Land and crops currently used for feeding people will be needed for the production of biofuels. In addition, growing crops requires nitrogen fertilisers and ploughing, harvesting and processing, all of which use energy mostly provided by burning fossil fuels.

Which one of the following statements best expresses the main conclusion of the above argument?

A   5.75% of biofuels used in petrol and diesel will significantly reduce global warming.

B   Using too much land and crops for biofuels will result in food shortages.

C   Biofuels may not necessarily help tackle global warming.

D   Alternative crop production methods are necessary to reduce carbon emissions.

E   The carbon use reduction targets on all countries is obligatory.

37   A round box of chocolates with a diameter of 40 cm and a depth of 3 cm is gift wrapped and tied with a 250 cm length of ribbon which is tied in a bow on top as shown below. After completion of the gift wrapping 60 cm of ribbon was left.

Bottom   Side   Top

A second piece of ribbon also measuring 250 cm is used to decorate a second gift. The ribbon is tied in a similar bow to the first gift and all the ribbon is used.

How many boxes of chocolates are there in the second gift?

A   6

B   10

C   5

D   4

E   12

38   What causes the level of the alternating rise and fall of the seas and oceans known as tides? The answer is, the gravitational pull of the moon and the sun on the rotating earth. It is the gravitational pull of the moon on the earth which keeps the earth in its monthly orbit, and as it is closer to earth than the sun it has twice the effect on the tides.

Which one of the following is the best statement of the flaw in the above argument?

A   It does not take into account the profound effect the weather can have on the tide.

B   It ignores the fact that some areas only have one tide.

C   The assumption made is one of cause and effect.

D   It overlooks spring tides when the lunar and solar tides line up.

E   It ignores the fact that strong winds and abnormal atmospheric pressure makes it impossible to predict tide levels.

39   A game has two bags of balls. Bag 'A' contains four red balls and four blue balls. Bag 'B' contains four red bats and four blue bats.

To play a game you have to have a matching red bat and red ball which are drawn from the bags whilst blindfolded. To achieve this, what is the *least* number of bats and balls you must draw from the bags?

A   Five balls and one bat.

B   Three balls and three bats.

C   Four balls and four bats.

D   Five balls and four bats.

E   Five balls and five bats.

40   The Supreme Court of the United Kingdom is composed of twelve British judges with the title of 'Justices of the Supreme Court'. Apart from exceptional cases such as those of high constitutional or great public importance, the Justices almost always sit as a panel of five with many decisions decided by a majority of three to two. Hence important cases are often decided by just three of the top twelve judges. In the United States' Supreme Court there are a total of nine Justices who hear all cases. There are often 5–4 splits in decisions but five is a larger majority of the judges compared with the British three out of twelve. The UK system is currently seen by many as a lottery and the fact that the outcome may also be dependent on the identity of the individual Justices involved. Considerable pressure is mounting for an increase in the number of Justices hearing appeals; with at the very least a majority of the total involved in important cases.

Which one of the following statements could be implied from this passage?

A   The UK should adopt the US system of having nine Justices.

B   Justices' decisions should ideally be based on a majority of their total number.

C   Decisions of the Justices would be improved by a US-style system.

D   Appeal decisions will always be influenced by the identity of the Justices on the panel.

E   In the UK decisions in appeals are decided by a panel of five Justices.

41 Below is a table detailing golf buggy hire.

TIGER GOLF CLUB
Summer buggy hire
7 am – 8 pm, 7 days per week

HOURLY RATE	
7 am – 5 pm	£3.50 per hour
5 pm – 8 pm	£2.25 per hour
½ day hire 7 am – 1 pm	£16.00
All day hire	£20.00
Refundable deposit £20.00	

How much will it cost to hire a golf buggy from 2 pm for 5 hours?

A   £17.50

B   £16.00

C   £15.00

D   £20.00

E   £11.25

42 The death rate of men in routine occupations in the North East of England is nearly four times that of those in higher managerial and professional occupations in the South East, according to research. The Office for National Statistics found that men in routine occupations – such as cleaners and labourers – in the North East had the highest death rate among men in all socio-economic groups and regions in England and Wales, at 699 per 100,000 men aged 25–64. Men in higher managerial and professional occupations – such as company directors and lawyers – in the South East (excluding London) had the lowest rate, at 179 per 100,000.

Which one of the following statements can be concluded from this report?

A   The death rate of company directors and lawyers in the North East is the same as their colleagues in the South East.

B   Socio-economic groups may only be one of the factors affecting higher mortality rates in the North East.

C   The death rate of professional people in the North East is higher than for managers in the South East.

D   Female cleaners in the North East and South East have lower death rates than men in the same areas.

> **E** Male lawyers working in London have a higher death rate than their colleagues in the North East.

43 June is helping her dad pack bait for his pest control business. The bait is in 10 g packets. June asks her dad how many packets of bait he needs. Her dad informs her that he sets 20 traps and places 20 g of bait in each trap. He works an 8 hour day and he checks all the traps every hour. During the first 5 hours he has to add 10 g of bait to half the traps each hour. During the last 3 hours he has to add 5 g of bait to three-quarters of the traps. If there is a part packet left he adds it to the last trap.

How many packets of bait does June need to pack for her dad?

A 58

B 37.5

C 38

D 57.5

E 60

44 Some commentators would suggest that the spread of sexually transmitted diseases (STDs) has reached almost pandemic proportions, increasing year on year since accurate records were first kept. However, with the exception of AIDS, almost all such diseases are now 'treatable' and have little or no long-term consequences on individual health and well-being. It has been argued that because STDs, apart from AIDS, are of limited risk to health, and their social stigma having lessened over time, public health authorities are failing to meet their obligations in adequately resourcing educational programmes designed to reduce or eliminate STDs.

Which one of the following statements, if true, would detract from the above argument?

A The number of people contracting STDs will decrease in the future.

B Providing educational resources for health management is expensive.

C National Health Service Trusts have increased expenditure on STD educational programmes at the same level as AIDS programmes.

D The social stigma attached to people who contract STDs will diminish over time.

E Further scientific advances will reduce the medical interventions required for people with STDs.

45 A cube has sides that each measure 40 cm in length.

What is the volume of the cube?

A 0.064 m

B 0.064 m^2

C 0.16 m^2

D 64,000 cm^3

E 1,600 cm^2

46 Mortgage lenders have been reducing the amount of funds available for some time. If, as predicted, the recession bites harder then the housing market is likely to be hit even more. As a result first-time buyers will have greater difficulty getting on the property ladder. Therefore, if the recession continues and mortgages become even tighter then first-time house buyers will be badly hit.

Which one of the following statements most closely mirrors the reasoning of the above argument?

A If the present level of storm and flood damage does not end soon then insurance companies will be inundated with claims. Some insurance companies may struggle to meet the level of claims and payments could take some time. If storm and flood damage become a feature of our climate insurance companies may add extra clauses to policies.

B If the cost of fuel continues to rise, then people will be more economical and will buy less fuel. The fuel prices will then stop increasing if less fuel is purchased. Therefore, the rise in fuel prices must peak soon.

C If we do not pay our skilled workers more, many of them will seek work abroad. We will then be left with a national skills shortage. Therefore, wages for skilled workers must increase if we wish to maintain a high skills base in this country.

D If we are all prepared to pay more road tax, then the government could afford to improve the road network. An improved road network would result in shorter more cost effective transport. Therefore, if we want a more efficient road system, we must be prepared to pay higher road tax.

E The UK car industry has been downsizing for some time. If the industry continues to decrease job losses will be high. Towns and cities whose economies depend on the salaries of car workers would suffer as a consequence. If the decline in the car industry continues then these towns and cities will be badly affected.

47 Jane buys biscuits once a fortnight for her grandmother. Her grandmother's favourite biscuits are 96p per packet and she gives Jane enough money for her usual fortnightly supply. At the supermarket there is a multi-buy offer on 10 packets or more. This reduces the packets by 16p each and Jane realises that her grandmother can now have two more packets of biscuits.

How many packets of biscuits does she buy?

A   10

B   12

C   14

D   16

E   20

48 This is an extract of a case to be heard by an employment tribunal.

A brokering company recently paid a €10 million out of court settlement to two Muslim women on race discrimination and sexual harassment grounds. Part of the settlement related to the company allocating staff on the basis of race specifically in regard to transferring the two Muslim women away from dealing with male Jewish clients. This case highlighted the difficulty for employers in reconciling client needs with their obligations to staff. The lawyers in the case urged the government to address this issue in any future equality legislation.

Which one of the following statements can be concluded from this extract?

A   Companies need to be aware of their obligations to employees before making blanket policies.

B   The customer is always right and should be able to determine whom they will deal with on a business basis.

C   The government is responsible for ensuring discrimination legislation reflects companies' working practices.

D   Had the Jewish clients been female then there would have been no case of sexual harassment.

E   Company policies may contain procedures that allow for positive discrimination in politically sensitive situations.

49 I am having friends round this evening for a barbeque. Some of my friends are vegetarian and I can't cook their veggie burgers and veggie sausages with the meat ones. We are due to eat at 7.00 pm and I have drawn up a timed 'To Do' list as follows:

> 'TO DO' LIST
>
> Make beef burgers and skewer sausages 15 minutes
>
> Barbeque beef burgers and sausages 30 minutes
>
> Cut bread rolls 10 minutes
>
> Make salad dressing 10 minutes
>
> Wash salad 5 minutes
>
> Toss salad in dressing 5 minutes
>
> Make veggie burgers and veggie sausages 30 minutes
>
> Barbeque veggie burgers and veggie sausages 30 minutes
>
> Put veggie food in hot store 5 minutes
>
> Put out patio furniture and lay the table 15 minutes

My barbeque has one grill area and an area for storing hot food. I will serve the food as soon as the meat burgers and sausages are cooked.

What is the latest time I should start preparing the food?

A 5.10 pm

B 5.25 pm

C 5.30 pm

D 4.25 pm

E 5.20 pm

50 Life after death has been a topic of considerable significance not only to the many religions of the world but also at an individual level. No more is this apparent than in the so-called 'spirit world', a world populated by 'mediums', those people who purport to communicate between the dead and their living relations and friends. These relations and friends are essentially individuals seeking solace and comfort in their difficult periods of grieving as they attempt to come to terms with their loss. Mediums are probably no less preposterous than fortune-tellers or astrologers, or even the person who reads your future in the tea leaves at the bottom of your cup.

Which one of the following statements is an underlying assumption of the above argument?

A   All religions believe in reincarnation.

B   Mediums can make contact with people who are dead.

C   Those who believe in the spirit world are often relatives of the recently bereaved.

D   Mediums, fortune-tellers and astrologers have extra-sensory perception.

E   Talking to dead loved ones is a comfort to surviving relations and friends.

16. Thinking Skills Assessment: answers and rationale

Below are the correct answers to the 50 multiple-choice questions. A full explanation of the rationale for both the correct and incorrect answers follows in the next section.

Question	Answer	Question	Answer
1	A	26	C
2	C	27	B
3	D	28	D
4	D	29	E
5	B	30	D
6	A	31	A
7	B	32	D
8	D	33	D
9	B	34	A
10	C	35	B
11	E	36	C
12	C	37	A
13	D	38	C
14	B	39	E
15	E	40	B
16	E	41	C
17	C	42	C
18	B	43	A
19	C	44	A
20	D	45	D
21	D	46	E
22	C	47	B
23	A	48	A
24	B	49	B
25	D	50	E

Rationale for correct and incorrect answers

1   This question relates to the passage on page 34.

From the indicated findings of this study it can be implied that:

A   the communication skills of children can be affected by reading.

B   children who read comics are better at public speaking.

C   children who read books are likely to be more creative compared to those who don't read books.

D   a child's communication skills are influenced by the type of comic they read.

E   it is generally accepted that girls are better communicators than boys in their teenage years.

Question 1: answer and rationale

To be **implied** means something that can be suggested but not overtly expressed; the act of reading between the lines or otherwise understanding a message that is implicit. You need to read the passage carefully to identify the overall argument and determine which one option best answers the question posed. The highlighted statement and rationale is correct.

A   the communication skills of children can be affected by reading.

This is the correct answer as the study clearly shows that children who regularly read comics are much better communicators compared with those who do not read comics. Even though the study was limited to children aged 12 to 15 years by implication the findings would equally apply to children outside this age range.

B   children who read comics are better at public speaking.

This is an incorrect answer as although the study found that children who read comics were better communicators compared with those who did not read comics, it cannot be implied that they may be better at 'public speaking' which may need skills other than simply being a good communicator.

C   children who read books are likely to be more creative compared to those who don't read books.

This is an incorrect answer as the study specifically relates to comics and not books. It may be that a comic's content, structure, etc., is such that it aids the development of communication skills and/or creativity. More information would be required to ascertain if this equally applied to books.

D   a child's communication skills are influenced by the type of comic they read.

This is an incorrect answer as nothing in the passage identifies a particular type of comic that would improve communication skills compared to another type of comic and therefore more information would be required.

E   it is generally accepted that girls are better communicators than boys in their teenage years.

This is an incorrect answer, as even though it has been shown in other research that teenage girls are often more socially aware and better communicators than boys of the same age, this is not contained within the passage and further information would be required.

2   A very successful scientific research company has appointed a design and marketing agency to come up with a new name for their company. They want a name that relates strongly to their professional ethos and business area. In addition, they want a name that can be displayed in their office and vehicle windows that will read the same vertically when viewed from inside or outside.

Which of the following names would suit their requirement?

A   MAXIM

B   MATRIX

C   AXIOM

D   WHICH

E   ATOM

Question 2: answer and rationale

This question requires that you can visualise the words written vertically and flipped horizontally to form a mirror image. Answers to this type of question can be rapidly eliminated when they contain letters that are not symmetrical, for example, the letter R and C when viewed as a mirror image would be 'Я' and 'Ɔ' therefore any answers containing these letters can be dismissed. Another requirement of this question is that you can understand the meaning of the words in order to select the most appropriate name for the company given their business area. The highlighted statement and rationale is correct.

A   MAXIM

This answer is incorrect, even though the letters are symmetrical, as the meaning of the word 'general principle deduced from experience' does not suit the requirement.

B MATRIX

This answer is incorrect as it contains the letter 'R' which, as a mirror image, would be 'Я' when viewed from the other side of a window.

C AXIOM

This answer is correct as it would read the same when viewed vertically from both inside and outside of a window, and the meaning of the word 'an accepted principle or assumption such as those upon which sciences are based' would be suitable for the scientific research company.

D WHICH

This answer is incorrect as it contains the letter 'C' which as a mirror image would be 'Ɔ ' when viewed from the other side of a window.

E ATOM

This answer is incorrect, even though the letters are symmetrical, as the meaning of the word 'the smallest portion of an element' does not suit the requirement.

3   J & B Engineering Limited undertook a validation study in order to determine the relationship between their recruitment tests and job performance (JP). The approximate overlaps of the tests with JP are as follows: numerical (N) 50%; verbal (V) 20%; Abstract (A) 33%. V and N also overlap with each other by 15% and V and N overlap with A by 33%.

Which one of the following Venn diagrams depicts this information?

A

B

C

D

E

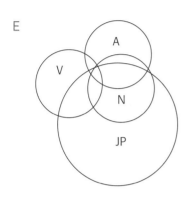

Question 3: answer and rationale

This question requires an examination of the diagrams to identify which can be eliminated immediately. The remaining diagrams then need to be examined closely to check for the right percentages of overlap between the tests themselves and the overlap each has with job performance. Venn diagrams are not always an exact science and you may be looking for the closest match to the data. The highlighted statement and rationale is correct.

A

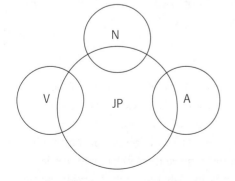

This answer is incorrect and can be dismissed immediately as the question clearly states that there is overlap between the three tests.

B

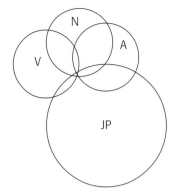

This answer is incorrect and can be dismissed fairly quickly as it is stated in the question that the numerical test (N) has a 50% overlap with job performance which would require the (N) circle to overlap approximately half with JP, which it does not.

C

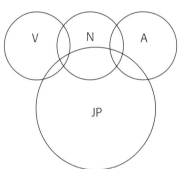

This answer is incorrect but needs more examination before it can be dismissed. The question states that both the Verbal (V) and Numerical (N) tests overlap with the Abstract (A) test by 33% and it can be seen from the diagram that the (V) test has no overlap at all with the (A) test.

D

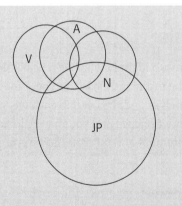

This answer is correct. The question asks that the numerical test (N) overlaps with JP by 50% and it can be seen in the diagram that the (N) test does overlap roughly 50%. Verbal (V) should overlap with JP 20%, which it roughly does. Abstract (A) should overlap with JP 33%, which it roughly does. V and N should overlap with each other by 15%, which they roughly do. Finally, V and N should both overlap with A by 33%, which they roughly do.

E

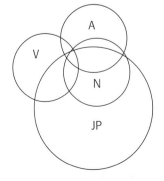

This answer is incorrect and can be dismissed fairly quickly as it is stated in the question that the numerical test (N) has a 50% overlap with job performance which would require the (N) circle to overlap approximately half with JP and it can be seen from the diagram that the overlap is closer to 80%.

4 This question relates to the passage on page 35.

Which one of the following statements is based on a similar principle to the TV licence argument?

A People with high incomes should not receive child benefit.

B Frequent travellers using bus, train or plane should pay less than occasional travellers.

C People who earn more should subsidise those who earn less so that they can afford private health care.

D Road tax is unfair for someone who has low mileage and we should be charged road tax on mileage bandings.

E Free bus passes should be means tested.

Question 4: *answer and rationale*

This question requires that you can identify when similar principles are being applied to two separate arguments. This requires an evaluation of the first argument in order to identify the basic premise. This premise can then be applied to each of the options to identify if there is any similarity. The highlighted statement and rationale is correct.

A People with high incomes should not receive child benefit.

This answer is incorrect as the basic premise of the argument in the passage is that you should only pay proportionately for what you are receiving. The above statement based on this premise could be argued to be the opposite as those on higher income are probably paying more into the benefit system and should perhaps receive more child benefit.

B Frequent travellers using bus, train or plane should pay less than occasional travellers.

This answer is incorrect based on the above premise as frequent travellers are receiving exactly the same as occasional travellers in terms of service. The argument in the passage is not based on how long you watch or don't watch the BBC but on whether you use the service at all.

C People who earn more should subsidise those who earn less so that they can afford private health care.

This answer is incorrect as the basic premise of the argument in the passage is that you should only pay proportionately for what you are receiving. The above statement based on this premise could be argued to be the opposite as those on higher income would be paying more to enable those who are earning less and paying less to receive the same level of private health care.

> **D**   Road tax is unfair for someone who has low mileage and we should be charged road tax on mileage bandings.
>
> This answer is the correct answer. The road tax system does appear to be inequitable to those who use the road systems less. As a proportion of road tax is spent on maintenance and increases in the network to cope with increased travel it does seem unfair to those who use the networks less.

E   Free bus passes should be means tested.

This answer is incorrect based on the above premise as those with higher incomes and who are potentially paying more into the system would not receive a free bus pass.

5   Magic Books Ltd publishes a range of children's books. Their books range from short to long text and they always have an illustration on the centre fold. The books range in size from 16 pages upwards but they are always in multiples of 16 pages, e.g. 16, 32, 48, 64 . . . Page one of the book is always the front cover.

The illustration on the centre fold could have which one of the following page numbering?

A   23 and 24

B   64 and 65

C   14 and 15

D   63 and 64

E   78 and 79

Question 5: answer and rationale

Book page sequencing: rule
The highlighted statement and rationale is correct.

A   23 and 24

This answer is incorrect and can be dismissed immediately as no matter how many pages there are in the book if the front cover is always counted as 1 then any odd number will be the right hand page of any fold. Therefore the first number of the centre fold has to be an even number.

B   64 and 65

This answer is correct. Firstly, it meets the criteria stated above. The second criterion is that the centre fold will be the middle two numbers of the total number of pages. Therefore, if a book has 16 pages then the centre fold would be pages 8 and 9, leaving seven pages either side. If the book has 32 pages the centre fold would be 16 and 17; 48 pages would be 24 and 25 and so on. Therefore, the left hand page of the centre fold would have to be divisible by 8.

C   14 and 15

This answer is incorrect. It meets the first criteria of an even number on the left hand page but as stated in the example above the left hand page of the centre fold would have to be divisible by 8.

D   63 and 64

This answer is incorrect and can be dismissed immediately as no matter how many pages there are in the book if the front cover is always counted as 1 then any odd number will be the right hand page of any fold. Therefore the first number of the centre fold has to be an even number.

E   78 and 79

This answer is incorrect. It meets the first criteria of an even number on the left hand page but as stated in the example above the left hand page of the centre fold would have to be divisible by 8.

6   This question relates to the passage on page 36.

Which one of the following is an underlying assumption of the above argument?

A   Entrance qualifications are a poor predictor of future attainment.

B   Degree results are prone to fluctuation.

C   English degrees are easier at Oxford and Cambridge.

D   Oxford and Cambridge attract students with higher potential.

E   Oxford and Cambridge attract the best lecturers.

Question 6: *answer and rationale*

An **assumption** is a proposition that is taken for granted, that is, as if it were known to be true. It is a statement that can be surmised or postulated given the overall context of the passage. This question is asking you to identify which statement can be surmised or postulated from the passage. In identifying an **assumption** the correct statement will not actually be stated in the passage so it is for you to determine the main argument and look for the reasoning to support this conclusion. You need to read the passage carefully to identify the overall argument and determine which one option best answers the question posed. The highlighted statement and rationale is correct.

A Entrance qualifications are a poor predictor of future attainment.

This is the correct answer as even though the degree requirements are almost identical, the '. . . research indicates a clear parity with Oxford and Cambridge in entrance qualifications with over 30% of other universities.'

B Degree results are prone to fluctuation.

This is an incorrect answer as there is nothing in the passage that suggests degree results are prone to fluctuation.

C English degrees are easier at Oxford and Cambridge.

This is an incorrect answer as the passage states that '. . . the degree requirements are almost identical' (with other universities).

D Oxford and Cambridge attract students with higher potential.

This is an incorrect answer as there is nothing within the passage that suggests Oxford and Cambridge attract students with higher potential. The passage does state that there is '. . . a clear parity with Oxford and Cambridge in entrance qualifications with over 30% of other universities.' Although it might be that students with higher potential apply to Oxford and Cambridge this cannot be assumed with the information provided.

E Oxford and Cambridge attract the best lecturers.

This is an incorrect answer as there is nothing in the passage that indicates the quality or otherwise of university staff whether in English or any other subject.

7 EnergyHeat and Warmhomes provide electricity on the following basis: EnergyHeat has a standing charge of £30 per quarter and charges 15p per kWh; Warmhomes has a standing charge of £24 per quarter and charges 20p per kWh.

How many kWh would you have to use in 1 month for the cost to be the same with both companies, calculating the standing charge pro rata?

A   30 kWh

B   40 kWh

C   50 kWh

D   60 kWh

E   70 kWh

Question 7: answer and rationale

Multi-stage calculations: rule

This question contains multiplication and addition.

The highlighted statement and rationale is correct.

A   30 kWh

This answer is incorrect as the costs would be £14.50 and £14 respectively.

B   40 kWh

This is the correct answer.

Step1: gather all the relevant information: EnergyHeat has a standing charge of £30 per quarter and charges 15p per kWh; Warmhomes has a standing charge of £24 per quarter and charges 20p per kWh.

Step 2: calculate the 1 month standing charges: EnergyHeat £30 ÷ 3 = £10 and Warmhomes £24 ÷ 3 = £8. Therefore there is a difference of £2.

Step 3: calculate the difference in kWh charge: 20p – 15p = 5p.

Step 4: calculate how many kWh at 5p could be purchased for the £2 difference = 40 and this provides a shortcut to the answer.

Therefore, 40 kWh with each company would cost the same with 1 month's pro rata standing charge.

C   50 kWh

This answer is incorrect as the costs would be £17.50 and £18 respectively.

D   60 kWh

This answer is incorrect as the costs would be £19 and £20 respectively.

E   70 kWh

This answer is incorrect as the costs would be £20.50 and £22 respectively.

8   This question relates to the passage on page 37.

Which one of the following statements can be implied from the passage?

A   The think-tank's deliberations do not consider the current economic climate.

B   Single parents forced into employment would benefit from higher childcare payments.

C   Single mothers who were forced to find work would be better off.

D   Benefit payments could be withdrawn from those refusing to seek work.

E   Higher maternity leave payments would benefit single mothers following their child's birth.

Question 8: *answer and rationale*

To be **implied** means something that can be suggested but not overtly expressed; the act of reading between the lines or otherwise understanding a message that is implicit. You need to read the passage carefully to identify the overall argument and determine which one option best answers the question posed. The highlighted statement and rationale is correct.

A   The think-tank's deliberations do not consider the current economic climate.

This is an incorrect answer as there is nothing in the passage that indicates whether or not the think-tank's deliberations consider the current economic climate.

B   Single parents forced into employment would benefit from higher childcare payments.

This is an incorrect answer as although the passage states 'Savings in benefits under the shake-up would be used to help fund universal childcare . . .' it is not clear whether the think-tank is recommending an increase in childcare benefits or actually funding childcare for everyone.

C   Single mothers who were forced to find work would be better off.

This is an incorrect answer as no details are contained in the passage of the benefit payments received by single mothers nor is there any indication of what they might earn in employment in order to make any form of comparison.

> **D**   Benefit payments could be withdrawn from those refusing to seek work.
>
> This is the correct answer as it is clearly implied at the beginning of the passage. The first sentence states 'The government is considering forcing single parents of children as young as two to seek work . . .', and the second sentence commences 'Savings in benefits under the shake-up . . .'. It is clear from these two statements that benefit payments could be withdrawn from those refusing to seek employment.

E   Higher maternity leave payments would benefit single mothers following their child's birth.

This is an incorrect answer as although such payments would benefit single mothers, it would only apply to those who had been in employment prior to giving birth.

9   The gemstone table below details the hardness, refractive index, and relative density of various gems.

GEMSTONE	HARDNESS	REFRACTIVE INDEX	RELATIVE DENSITY
Alexandrite	8.5	1.746–1.763	3.70–3.78
Amber	2.5	1.539–1.545	1.05–1.09
Citrine	7.0	1.544–1.533	2.65
Emerald	8.0	1.565–1.602	2.67–2.78
Diamond	10.0	2.417–2.419	3.50–3.53
Ruby	9.0	1.762–1.778	3.97–4.05
Sapphire	9.0	1.762–1.788	3.95–4.03
Tanzanite	7.0	1.691–1.700	3.35
Topaz	8.0	1.609–1.643	3.49–3.57
Zircon	7.5	1.810–2.024	3.93–4.73

What are the mean value of hardness and the mode value of relative density (using the highest value from the range where necessary)?

A   7.65 and 3.57

B   7.65 and 3.55

C   7.75 and 3.55

D   7.65 and 3.53

E   7.5 and 3.55

Question 9: *answer and rationale*

Mean, mode and range: rule

This question requires an understanding of mean, mode and range and the ability to perform the necessary calculations.

The highlighted statement and rationale is correct.

A   7.65 and 3.57

This answer is incorrect as the mode value of relative density is incorrect; 3.57 should have been added to 3.53 and divided by 2 to arrive at the mode value of 3.55.

B   7.65 and 3.55

This is the correct answer.

Step 1: calculate the mean value of hardness by adding all the values and dividing by 10.

So: 8.5 + 2.5 + 7.0 + 8.0 + 10.0 + 9.0 + 9.0 + 7.0 + 8.0 + 7.5 = 76.5 ÷ 10 = 7.65 mean value.

Step 2: calculate the mode value of relative density using the highest value from the range where necessary.

So: order the values from lowest to highest: 1.09, 2.65, 2.78, 3.35, 3.53, 3.57, 3.78, 4.03, 4.05, 4.73 and, as there are an even number of values, take the middle two values 3.53 + 3.57 = 7.10 ÷ 2 = 3.55 mode value of relative density.

Therefore the mean value of hardness and mode value of relative density are 7.65 and 3.55.

C   7.75 and 3.55

This answer is incorrect as the mean value has been calculated incorrectly; 7.75 is the mode value of hardness.

D   7.65 and 3.53

This answer is incorrect as the mode value of relative density is incorrect; 3.53 should have been added to 3.57 and divided by 2 to arrive at the mode value of 3.55.

E   7.5 and 3.55

This answer is incorrect as the mean value has been calculated incorrectly; 7.5 is the range value of hardness.

10   This question relates to the passage on page 38.

Which one of the following statements best summarises the main conclusion of the above argument?

  A   The world is likely to end due to air travel.

  B   A ban on planes would reduce pollution.

  C   The problem of aircraft emissions and the number of flights needs to be resolved.

  D   Aircraft flights cause changes to the world climate.

  E   Cut-price flights and the increasing number of airlines are to blame for global warming.

Question 10: *answer and rationale*

This question requires that you can identify the **main conclusion** of the argument presented in the passage. This is an evaluation as to whether or not the options provided are the main conclusion, in other words are they true or false in relation to the question. In order to address this question it will be necessary to read the passage thoroughly in order to follow the ideas and structure of the argument to reach the main conclusion. The passage may contain several points that are pertinent to the overall argument as they help to build up the body of evidence. The highlighted statement and rationale is correct.

  A   The world is likely to end due to air travel.

This is an incorrect answer. The passage states that air travel is a major contributor to global warming and that it may be detrimental to the survival of Earth but it cannot be concluded that it will result in the end of the world.

  B   A ban on planes would reduce pollution.

This is an incorrect answer. The passage states that the level of pollution from air travel is high and therefore it could be concluded that a ban on planes would reduce pollution. However, this is not suggested in the passage and is therefore not the main conclusion.

  C   The problem of aircraft emissions and the number of flights needs to be resolved.

This is the correct answer as the passage builds an argument based on the increased number of flights and the subsequent increased levels of pollution. The passage states that air travel must be regulated and the obvious conclusion to be drawn is that aircraft emissions and the number of flights needs to be resolved to facilitate this.

  D   Aircraft flights cause changes to the world climate.

This is an incorrect answer as it is only part of the argument put forward in the passage and purely a contributory factor to the main conclusion.

E   Cut-price flights and the increasing number of airlines are to blame for global warming.

This is an incorrect answer. Cut-price flights and the increasing number of airlines may have added to global warming but they are not the only contributors. This again is only a contributory factor to the main conclusion.

11   A farmer owns land that totals 254 acres. His house and personal garden take up 1.75 acres, barns and other farm buildings take up 2.25 acres. The remaining land is split between 60% pasture land and 40% arable. The farmer always rests a quarter of his arable land each year, 4% is taken up by tracks and hedges and 1% fails to yield any crops.

What is the acreage of productive arable land in a year?

A   100 acres

B   105 acres

C   30 acres

D   75 acres

E   70 acres

Question 11: answer and rationale

Calculations using percentages and fractions: rule

This question contains multiplication and addition using percentages and fractions.

The highlighted statement and rationale is correct.

A   100 acres

This answer is incorrect as it has failed to subtract the 30% of land (¼ or 25% land rested, 4% tracks and hedges and 1% failed yield) that fails to yield any crops.

B   105 acres

This answer is incorrect as it has based the calculations on the 60% of pasture land and not the 40% of arable land.

C   30 acres

This answer is incorrect as it has used the 30% of land (¼ or 25% land rested, 4% tracks and hedges and 1% failed yield) that fails to yield any crops instead of the remaining 70%.

D   75 acres

This answer is incorrect as it has only subtracted the ¼ or 25% of land rested.

E 70 acres

This is the correct answer.

Step 1: Calculate the amount of pasture and arable land: 254 − 1.75 + 2.25 = 250.

Step 2: Calculate 40% of the land to arrive at the arable acreage: $250 \times \frac{40}{100} = 100$ acres.

Step 3: Subtract the 30% of land (¼ or 25% land rested, 4% tracks and hedges and 1% failed yield).

Therefore we are left with 70% of 100 acres that equates easily to 70 acres.

12 This question relates to the passage on page 39.

Which one of the following statements best identifies the flaw in the above argument?

A Campaigners can influence the voting patterns of the British public.

B Elected candidates could resign whichever way the vote goes.

C A high percentage of the public do not vote and we can never be sure what impact their votes would have on the result.

D The system of voting in Britain is unfair and we should change to a system of proportional representation.

E Voters can change their minds regularly and therefore results are not predictable.

Question 12: answer and rationale

This question requires that you can identify the **flaw** in the argument presented in the passage. This is an evaluation as to whether or not the options provided best describe the flaw in the argument, in other words are they true or false in relation to the question. In order to address this question it will be necessary to read the passage thoroughly in order to reach a conclusion as to which option would constitute the main flaw in the argument. The options may all appear feasible but you must decide which one option would question the whole premise. The highlighted statement and rationale is correct.

A Campaigners can influence the voting patterns of the British public.

This is an incorrect answer as it is clearly stated in the passage that the strength of the campaign can influence voters.

B Elected candidates could resign whichever way the vote goes.

This is an incorrect answer. This could be problematic for those who voted for a candidate who resigns but it is not the main flaw in the above argument.

> **C** A high percentage of the public do not vote and we can never be sure what impact their votes would have on the result.

This is the correct answer as the passage states that 'the new party will have the support of the majority of the eligible voting public' which is incorrect as a high percentage do not vote and therefore the impact of their vote is unknown.

D The system of voting in Britain is unfair and we should change to a system of proportional representation.

This is an incorrect answer. This statement may be a view supported by some of the voting public but it does not constitute a flaw in the argument put forward in the passage and is therefore irrelevant.

E Voters can change their minds regularly and therefore results are not predictable.

This is an incorrect answer as the prediction of results is not covered in the passage and is therefore irrelevant.

13 We have oil-fired central heating in our home and home office that we keep on during the months of October to March. We are allowed to allocate 20% of the bill as a business expense. Our oil tank has an electronic meter that shows the total litres used and we record this on the 1st of each month.

	LITRES USED
1 October	1058
1 November	1217
1 December	1399
1 January	1596
1 February	1815
1 March	2032

During which month did the home office use most oil?

A October

B February

C March

D January

E December

Question 13: answer and rationale

Calculations using subtraction: rule

This question contains subtraction. The percentage calculation is a red herring and is not required in order to arrive at the correct answer. The highest usage in any month will also include the highest 20%.

The highlighted statement and rationale is correct.

A October

This answer is incorrect as this month had the lowest usage of oil.

B February

This answer is incorrect but would need to be calculated as the total usage for this month is only 2 litres less, at 217 litres, than the highest at 219 litres.

C March

This answer is incorrect as the amount used for March will not be known until 1 April.

D January

This is the correct answer.

Step 1: Calculate the usage for each month: October's usage is 1217 – 1058 = 159, November's usage is 1399 – 1217 = 182, December's usage is 1596 – 1399 = 197, January's usage is 1815 – 1596 = 219 and February's usage is 2032 – 1815 = 217.

Therefore January has the highest usage.

E December

This answer is incorrect as this month had the third lowest usage of oil.

14 This question relates to the passage on page 40.

Which one of the following statements best expresses the conclusion of this argument?

   A Attracting new investors in business is difficult.

   B If dividends are not increased the business may not grow.

   C Shareholders will have to accept small dividends.

   D Top Ten Ltd may close due to a lack of expansion.

   E If dividends are increased the business will have more shareholders.

Question 14: *answer and rationale*

This question requires that you can identify the **main conclusion** of the argument presented in the passage. This is an evaluation as to whether or not the options provided are the main conclusion, in other words are they true or false in relation to the question. In order to address this question it will be necessary to read the passage thoroughly in order to follow the ideas and structure of the argument to reach the main conclusion. The passage may contain several points that are pertinent to the overall argument as they help to build up the body of evidence. The highlighted statement and rationale is correct.

A   Attracting new investors in business is difficult.

This answer is incorrect and is not a conclusion that can be drawn from the passage.

B   If dividends are not increased the business may not grow.

This answer is correct. The conclusion to be drawn from the passage is that new investors are needed in order for the business to expand. In order to attract new investors dividends need to be increased, therefore, if dividends are not increased the business may not grow.

C   Shareholders will have to accept small dividends.

This answer is incorrect even though it may be true if the business does not increase its dividends. However, the argument is clearly about business expansion and the impact dividends may have on this.

D   Top Ten Ltd may close due to a lack of expansion.

This answer is incorrect and is not suggested anywhere in the passage.

E   If dividends are increased the business will have more shareholders.

This answer is incorrect even though it is suggested in the passage that an increase in dividends will attract more shareholders. However, the argument is clearly about business expansion and the impact dividends may have on this.

15 The table below shows the number of males and females from a study of 100 people that purchase various types of insurance.

Male	Type of Insurance	Female
54	Car	36
44	Home	45
37	Contents	45
22	Health	17
9	Employment Protection	5
5	Travel	5
7	Sport	2
14	Pet	15
14	Dental	15
3	Business Liability	1

The average difference between the number of men and women that purchase Home, Sport and Dental insurance is?

A 3

B 2

C 5

D −1

E 1

Question 15: answer and rationale

Multiple calculations and average: rule

This question contains addition, subtraction and the calculation of the average.

The highlighted statement and rationale is correct.

A 3

This answer is incorrect as it is the total difference between the three areas of insurance not the average.

B 2

This answer is incorrect as it is the average difference between Sport and Dental insurance only.

C 5

This answer is incorrect as it is the difference between Sports insurance only.

D –1

This answer is incorrect as it is the difference between Home insurance only.

E 1

This is the correct answer.

Step 1: extract the relevant data from the table: Home, Sport and Dental insurance figures for males and females.

So males 44, 7, 14; females 45, 2, 15

Step 2: Add the amounts, males 44 + 7 + 14 = 65; females 45 + 2 + 15 = 62

Step 3: Subtract the amounts 65 – 62 = 3

Step 4: Calculate the average difference, 3 ÷ 3 areas of insurance = 1

16 This question relates to the passage on page 41.

Which one of the following statements is an underlying assumption of the above argument?

A   The cost of private health care is not a measure of its effectiveness.

B   The more you pay the better the health provision.

C   Private health care is no better than the National Health Service.

D   Individuals should be prepared to pay for health care.

E   Life expectancy is a reliable measure of the efficacy of private health care.

Question 16: answer and rationale

This question is asking you to determine which statement is an **assumption** made by the writer. An **assumption** is something that is proposed or implied in the passage. An **assumption** may not be expressed in the passage and may not be supported by fact, but it should be evident from the overall context of the passage. The highlighted statement and rationale is correct.

A   The cost of private health care is not a measure of its effectiveness.

This is an incorrect answer as it is explicitly stated in the passage that life expectancies are not significantly different no matter what is paid for health care.

B   The more you pay the better the health provision.

This is an incorrect answer as it is explicitly stated in the passage 'that you receive what you pay for is . . . irrelevant in terms of private health care'.

C   Private health care is no better than the National Health Service.

This is an incorrect answer as the passage does not imply that there is comparison between private health care and the National Health Service.

D   Individuals should be prepared to pay for health care.

This is an incorrect answer and is irrelevant in relation to the passage.

E   Life expectancy is a reliable measure of the efficacy of private health care.

This is the correct answer as the assumption behind the argument in the passage is that life expectancy is a reliable measure of the efficacy of private health care, indeed it is the only measure mentioned.

17 What is the volume of the following cuboid in cm³ ?

A   187500 cm³

B   18750 cm³

C   187.5 cm³

D   18.75 cm³

E   1875 cm³

Question 17: answer and rationale

Volume and the relationship between mm and cm: rule

This question requires the use of the formula for calculating the volume of a cuboid and the conversion of mm³ to cm³.

The highlighted statement and rationale is correct.

A   187500 cm³

This answer is incorrect as this figure would be the volume in mm³.

B   18750 cm³

This answer is incorrect as the mm³ have been divided by 10 instead of 1000.

C 187.5 cm^3

This is the correct answer.

Step 1: Calculate the volume of the cuboid = length × width × height

So 150 mm × 25 mm × 50 mm = 187500 mm^3

Step 2: Convert 187500 mm^3 to cm^3

So 1 cm^3 = 1000 mm^3, therefore 187500 ÷ 1000 = 187.5 cm^3.

D 18.75 cm^3

This answer is incorrect as the mm^3 have been divided by 10000 instead of 1000.

E 1875 cm^3

This answer is incorrect as the mm^3 have been divided by 100 instead of 1000.

18 This question relates to the passage on page 41.

Which one of the following is the best statement of the flaw in the passage above?

A Any number could be related to a series of facts.

B The use of these numbers has been chosen in some cases and could be coincidental in others.

C David Beckham has not always worn a number twenty-three shirt as he used to wear a number seven shirt.

D The links between some facts and the numbers are very tenuous.

E Twenty-three and forty-one are not prime numbers.

Question 18: *answer and rationale*

This question requires that you can identify the **flaw** in the argument presented in the passage. This is an evaluation as to whether or not the options provided best describe the flaw in the argument, in other words are they true or false in relation to the question. In order to address this question it will be necessary to read the passage thoroughly in order to reach a conclusion as to which option would constitute the main flaw in the argument. The options may all appear feasible but you must decide which one option would question the whole premise. The highlighted statement and rationale is correct.

A Any number could be related to a series of facts.

This is an incorrect answer as it would be difficult to associate lengthy numbers to a series of facts and even if true it is not the best example of the flaw in the argument.

> **B** The use of these numbers has been chosen in some cases and could be coincidental in others.
>
> This is the correct answer as it best describes the flaw in the argument. The fact that the two numbers mentioned have, in some instances, been specifically chosen and the possibility of coincidence questions the premise that these are more than numbers.

C David Beckham has not always worn a number twenty-three shirt as he used to wear a number seven shirt.

This is an incorrect answer as it only poses the flaw in one of the examples given in the passage and not the flaw in the whole argument.

D The links between some facts and the numbers are very tenuous.

This is an incorrect answer as the suggestion that some of the links are very tenuous does not invalidate the argument.

E Twenty-three and forty-one are not prime numbers.

This is an incorrect answer as 23 and 41 are prime numbers.

19 After dropping off their children at the local playgroup four mothers were discussing how many dolls each of their daughters had. The four daughters were aged 1, 2, 3 and 4 and they had one, two, three and four dolls but not necessarily respectively. Elizabeth has more dolls than her age. Sarah is older than Alisha. Only one girl has the same number of dolls as her age. Mia has fewer dolls than Sarah and the girl aged 3 has two dolls. Mia is the youngest.

How old is Alisha and how many dolls does she have?

A Alisha is 1 year old and she has four dolls.

B Alisha is 2 years old and she has two dolls.

C Alisha is 3 years old and she has two dolls.

D Alisha is 3 years old and she has three dolls.

E Alisha is 4 years old and she has one doll.

Question 19: *answer and rationale*

Dependent events and random: rule
This question is based on dependent events, in other words, the probabilities of the second event will be influenced by the outcomes of the first event and so on.

The highlighted statement and rationale is correct.

A   Alisha is 1 year old and she has four dolls.

This answer is incorrect as we know that Mia is the youngest.

B   Alisha is 2 years old and she has two dolls.

This answer is incorrect but the problem would need to be solved to discount this option.

C   Alisha is 3 years old and she has two dolls.

This is the correct answer.

Step 1: Tabulate the given information:

Name	Age	Number of Dolls
Mia	1	
	2	2
	3	4

Step 2: What can be deduced from the text: Deduction 1 – Elizabeth cannot be aged 3 or 4 as she has to have more dolls than her age so she must be aged 2 with either three or four dolls.

Name	Age	Number of Dolls
Mia	1	
Elizabeth	2	3/4
	3	2
	4	

Step 3: Sarah is older than Alisha; therefore Alisha is aged 3 and Sarah is aged 4.

Name	Age	Number of Dolls
Mia	1	
Elizabeth	2	3/4
Alisha	3	2
Sarah	4	

Step 4: Mia has fewer dolls than Sarah which would have to be one as only one girl has the same number of dolls as her age, and any other combination would not fit this requirement. Sarah must have three dolls and Elizabeth four. This step is given for information only.

Name	Age	Number of Dolls
Mia	1	1
Elizabeth	2	4
Alisha	3	2
Sarah	4	3

Therefore the answer could have been determined after *Step 3.*

D Alisha is 3 years old and she has three dolls.

This answer is incorrect but the problem would need to be solved to discount this option.

E Alisha is 4 years old and she has one doll.

This answer is incorrect but the problem would need to be solved to discount this option.

20 This question relates to the passage on page 42.

Which one of the following statements, if factual, would reduce the power of the above argument?

    A The internet is too graphic in its portrayal of knife crime.

    B Most people are unaware of the statistics of knife crime.

    C Knife crime has replaced other forms of violent crime.

    D Adults are less likely to access internet sites detailing knife crime.

    E Surveys have accurately identified the population's views on knife crime.

Question 20: *answer and rationale*

This question requires that you can identify which statement, **if factual**, would reduce the power of the argument presented in the passage. This is an evaluation as to whether the options provided, if they were true, would most weaken the argument. In order to address this question it will be necessary to read the passage thoroughly in order to arrive at the most logical answer. The options may all appear feasible but you must decide which one option would be the most likely. The highlighted statement and rationale is correct.

A The internet is too graphic in its portrayal of knife crime.

This is an incorrect answer as this statement supports the argument.

B Most people are unaware of the statistics of knife crime.

This is an incorrect answer. The passage states that those questioned as part of the survey were unaware of the actual statistics of knife crime. This, however, does not reduce the power of the argument for the removal of knife crime information from the internet.

C Knife crime has replaced other forms of violent crime.

This is an incorrect answer. There is no mention made in the passage about other forms of violent crime and this statement is irrelevant in terms of the question being asked.

> **D**   Adults are less likely to access internet sites detailing knife crime.

This is the correct answer. The passage argues that the main media for information about knives and knife crime is the internet and that these sites make it more fearful than it really is. The passage states that the fear is greater with adults even though the group most affected is young males. It could be realistically argued that the young males are more likely to access these sites than adults, therefore, the heightened fear amongst adults is perhaps generated from other sources than the internet. This would, if factual, reduce the power of the argument presented in the passage.

E   Surveys have accurately identified the population's views on knife crime.

This is an incorrect answer as the passage states that those surveyed over-estimated the likelihood of becoming a victim of knife crime. This may or may not generalise to the population as a whole and even if it does it is irrelevant in terms of the question posed.

21   Mum and Dad are taking their children to the cinema. Mum is taking the youngest child to see *Beauty and the Beast*, Dad is going to watch *Rocky V*, their teenage daughter is meeting her friends to watch *High School Musical*, and their twin boys are watching a cartoon hour followed by a game of ten-pin bowling. The Majestic Cinema and Bowling Alley listings are below.

The Majestic Cinema and Bowling Alley	
Ten-pin bowling	Hourly at a quarter to the hour Commencing 09.45 to 20.45 Duration 90 minutes
Rocky V	3 hourly at a quarter past the hour Commencing 16.15 to 19.15 Duration 2 hours 45 minutes
High School Musical	3 hourly at 20 past the hour Commencing 13.20 to 19.20 Duration 2 hours 15 minutes
Beauty and the Beast	3 hourly at a quarter to the hour Commencing 12.45 to 18.45 Duration 2 hours 5 minutes
Cartoon hour	On the hour Commencing 11.00 to 20.00

Mum and Dad are taking the whole family for a pizza afterwards. Mum and Dad want to begin watching the films as early as possible. What time do they need to arrive at the cinema, including 15 minutes to purchase tickets and drinks etc., and what is the earliest possible time they can meet in the foyer afterwards?

A   15.30 and 19.00

B   15.45 and 18.15

C   15.45 and 19.15

D   15.30 and 19.15

E   15.45 and 19.00

Question 21: answer and rationale

Extracting information and multi-stage calculations: rule

This question requires that you can extract the relevant information from a table and perform addition.

The highlighted statement and rationale is correct.

A   15.30 and 19.00

This answer is incorrect as the finish time is too early for the twins.

B   15.45 and 18.15

This answer is incorrect as the start time does not allow for 15 minutes for the purchase of tickets etc. and the finish time has been calculated 1 hour too early.

C   15.45 and 19.15

This answer is incorrect as the start time does not allow for 15 minutes for the purchase of tickets etc.

D   15.30 and 19.15

This is the correct answer.

Step 1: extract the relevant information: they need to be at the cinema 15 minutes before the earliest start time, Mum is taking the youngest child to see *Beauty and the Beast*, Dad is going to watch *Rocky V*, their teenage daughter is meeting her friends to watch *High School Musical*, their twin boys are watching a cartoon hour followed by a game of ten-pin bowling and they are all meeting for a pizza afterwards.

Step 2: calculate start and finishing times for all four sessions: Dad will have to attend the 16.15 show (the only other showing, 3 hours later, will be too late) therefore 16.15 + 2 hrs 45 mins = 19.00 finishing time, therefore the other start times will need to be as close as possible to 16.00 given the 15 minutes time to buy tickets etc.; Mum and the youngest daughter will have to attend the 15.45 showing of *Beauty and the Beast* as the other times available of 12.25 and 18.45 are too early and too late respectively, therefore 15.45 + 2 hrs 5 mins = 17.50 finishing time; the teenage daughter will have to attend the 16.20 showing of *High School Musical* as the other times available of 13.20 and 19.20 are too early and too late respectively, therefore 16.20 + 2 hrs 15 mins = 18.35; the twins will have to attend the 16.00 cartoon showing, therefore 16.00 + 1 hr = 17.00 and the next available bowling slot will be 17.45 + 90 mins (1 hr 30 mins) = 19.15.

Step 3: Therefore the earliest start time of 15.45 – 15 minutes for the purchase of tickets etc. = 15.30 and the latest finish time is 19.15.

E   15.45 and 19.00

This answer is incorrect as the start time does not allow for 15 minutes for the purchase of tickets etc. and the finish time is too early for the twins.

22 This question relates to the passage on page 44.

What main conclusion can be drawn from this passage?

A   The Olympic ideal has been lost at the expense of consumerism.

B   The Olympic Games in London is seeking to provide bigger and better venues than the previous Games in China.

C   Urban regeneration and other benefits may be the legacy of the Olympic Games in London's East End.

D   There has been a fivefold increase in the projected costs for hosting the Olympic Games in London compared to the original figure.

E   Part of the £9.35bn, the projected cost of hosting the Olympic Games, will be met by a post-Games economic boost.

Question 22: *answer and rationale*

This question requires that you can identify the **main conclusion** of the argument presented in the passage. This is an evaluation as to whether the options provided are the main conclusion or not, in other words, are they true or false in relation to the question. In order to address this question it will be necessary to read the passage thoroughly in order to follow the ideas and structure of the argument to reach the main conclusion. The passage may contain several points that are pertinent to the overall argument as they help to build up the body of evidence. The highlighted statement and rationale is correct.

A   The Olympic ideal has been lost at the expense of consumerism.

This is an incorrect answer as, in relation to this statement, the passage states 'The Olympic ideal is about the brotherhood of man but it now seems to be about each country outshining previous holders of the event in the splendour of its show.' Although many would agree with this statement there is no mention of 'consumerism', that is, a desire to purchase goods and services in ever greater amounts, contained in the passage.

B   The Olympic Games in London is seeking to provide bigger and better venues than the previous Games in China.

This is an incorrect answer as the only part of the passage that might relate to this statement is '. . . each country outshining previous holders of the event in the splendour of its show.' This does not specifically refer to venues and therefore further information would be required.

C   Urban regeneration and other benefits may be the legacy of the Olympic Games in London's East End.

This is the correct answer as the last sentence of the passage states 'This spurious form of national glory is defended by the palliative promises of a significant long-term economic boost for London's East End but it is believed these will fall far short of expectations.' This clearly refers to 'urban regeneration' but is doubtful that the economic boost will meet expectations, however, they may be the legacy of the Games.

D   There has been a fivefold increase in the projected costs for hosting the Olympic Games in London compared to the original figure.

This is an incorrect answer as the second sentence of the passage states 'The projected cost for the London Olympics was originally £2.4bn but this has now risen to £9.35bn.' A fivefold increase of the original costs would be £2.4bn × 5 = £12bn, clearly far more than the actual projected figure of £9.35bn.

E   Part of the £9.35bn, the projected cost of hosting the Olympic Games, will be met by a post-Games economic boost.

This is an incorrect answer as, although the first sentence refers to a profit made by the 1948 Games, there is nothing in the passage that suggests that any of the costs of the Games will be met by a post-Games economic boost.

23 The diagram below shows a round serviette which has three identical segments
    torn out from around the edge.

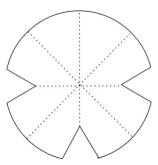

The dotted lines represent the folds of the serviette. Which one of the following
diagrams would not be possible once folded along any one of the folds?

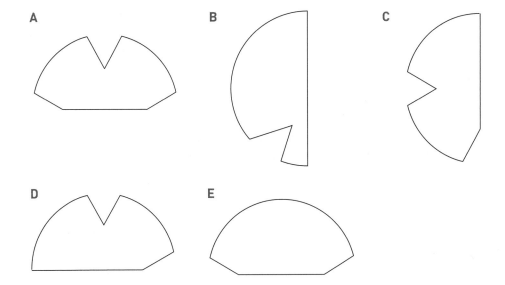

A

B

C

D

E

Question 23: *answer and rationale*

This question requires that you can use your spatial ability mentally to fold and rotate a
shape in order to arrive at the answer. Note the question is asking which shape **cannot** be
made. The highlighted statement and rationale is correct.

A

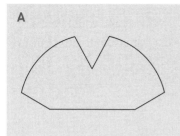

This is the correct answer as this shape cannot be made when the serviette is folded along one of the dotted lines. If the serviette were folded from bottom to top the full curve of the top of the circle would be visible through the segment. If it was folded from top to bottom and rotated 180° the cut out segment at the bottom of the diagram would not be visible. All of the other possible folds are irrelevant.

B

This is an incorrect answer as this shape could be made by folding the shape in the diagram diagonally from bottom right to top left and then rotating the shape 45° round to the right.

C

This is an incorrect answer as this shape could be made by folding the shape in the diagram over from right to left.

D

This is an incorrect answer as this shape could be made by folding the shape in the diagram over from left to right and then rotating the shape 90° to the left.

E This is an incorrect answer as this shape could be made by folding the shape in the diagram from top to bottom and then rotating the shape 180°.

24 This question relates to the passage on page 45.

Which one of the following best depicts the main conclusion of the above argument?

A   Food centres reduce the levels of waste.

B   Land can be used for local food businesses.

C   Locally produced food reduces the need for mass produced food.

D   Local food centres are preferable to supermarkets.

E   Small local food centres do not use as many resources as supermarkets.

Question 24: *answer and rationale*

This question requires that you can identify the **main conclusion** of the argument presented in the passage. This is an evaluation as to whether or not the options provided are the main conclusion, in other words are they true or false in relation to the question. In order to address this question it will be necessary to read the passage thoroughly in order to follow the ideas and structure of the argument to reach the main conclusion. The passage may contain several points that are pertinent to the overall argument as they help to build up the body of evidence. The highlighted statement and rationale is correct.

A   Food centres reduce the levels of waste.

This is an incorrect answer. The passage does make the point that the wasted packaging is less from food centres as opposed to supermarkets but it only forms part of the main conclusion.

B   Land can be used for local food businesses.

This is the correct answer as the passage builds an argument for the use of available building land being used for local food businesses as opposed to supermarkets due to the benefits to the environment and local economies.

C   Locally produced food reduces the need for mass produced food.

This is an incorrect answer and does not form part of the argument put forward in the passage. It could be assumed that this would be the case but it would be a weak conclusion to draw from the passage.

D Local food centres are preferable to supermarkets.

This is an incorrect answer even though it is a conclusion which could be drawn from the content of the passage. However, it does not take into account the use of future building land.

E Small local food centres do not use as many resources as supermarkets.

This is an incorrect answer albeit a part of the argument put forward in the passage. Again, this answer does not take into account the main points of the passage.

25 The following table shows the percentage fall in house value prices during the past 12 months as a result of the worldwide economic recession.

Percentage fall in world house prices	
Slovakia	−31%
Russia	−26%
Hong Kong	−18%
US	−15%
UK	−10%
Ireland	−8%
China	−5%
Germany	−3%
France	−2%
Spain	−2%

According to this table which of the following is true?

A The average percentage fall in house prices in EEC (Slovakia, UK, Ireland, Germany, France and Spain) is less than half that of the non-EEC countries shown.

B The percentage fall in the price of a house in the US is almost half that of Slovakia and more than twice that of Ireland.

C The average price of a house in Ireland has fallen less than the UK but more than China.

D The combined percentage fall of the bottom five countries in the table is less than the percentage fall in Russia alone.

E The combined percentage fall of the US, China and France is equal to that of Russia.

Question 25: *answer and rationale*

Percentages and multi-stage calculations: rule

This question requires the understanding of negative percentages and the ability to perform addition and subtraction.

The highlighted statement and rationale is correct.

A   The average percentage fall in house prices in EEC (Slovakia, UK, Ireland, Germany, France and Spain) is less than half that of the non-EEC countries shown.

This answer is incorrect. The average percentage fall in house prices in the EEC countries is: $-31 + -10 + -8 + -3 + -2 + -2 = -56$, divided by 6 (the number of countries) = -9.33%. The average percentage fall in house prices in the non-EEC countries is: $-26 + -18 + -15 + -5 = -64$, divided by 4 (the number of countries) = -16%. Therefore -9.33% is not less than half of -16%.

B   The percentage fall in the price of a house in the US is almost half that of Slovakia and more than twice that of Ireland.

This answer is incorrect. The percentage fall for the US at -15% is almost half that of Slovakia at -31%, but twice the percentage fall for Ireland would be -16%, which would be greater than the US fall.

C   The average price of a house in Ireland has fallen less than the UK but more than China.

This answer is incorrect. The average price of a house in Ireland at -8% has fallen more than China at -3% but the -10% for the UK is a larger drop than Ireland.

D   The combined percentage fall of the bottom five countries in the table is less than the percentage fall in Russia alone.

This is the correct answer.

Step 1: The combined percentage of the bottom five countries in the table (Ireland, China, Germany, France and Spain) is $-8\% + -5\% + -3\% + -2\% + -2\% = -20\%$ whereas Russia is -26%. Therefore the combined percentage fall is less than that for Russia.

E   The combined percentage fall of the US, China and France is equal to that of Russia.

This answer is incorrect. The combined percentage fall of the US, China and France is $-15\% + -5\% + -2\% = -22\%$ which is less than the fall of -26% for Russia.

26 This question relates to the passage on page 46.

Which one of the following conclusions can be drawn from the above passage?

A SSRIs are safer as a common form of suicide was to overdose on toxic antidepressants.

B Using alternative medicine such as St John's Wort is preferable to SSRIs.

C More extensive research needs to be undertaken by all concerned to extend the understanding of how antidepressants and depression affect the brain.

D The drugs used to treat depression are no better than placebos and should not be prescribed as freely as they are.

E The use of 'talking therapies' to treat depression would be more effective and safer than conventional drugs such as SSRIs.

Question 26: *answer and rationale*

This question requires that you can identify the **main conclusion** of the argument presented in the passage. This is an evaluation as to whether or not the options provided are the main conclusion, in other words are they true or false in relation to the question. In order to address this question it will be necessary to read the passage thoroughly in order to follow the ideas and structure of the argument to reach the main conclusion. The passage may contain several points that are pertinent to the overall argument as they help to build up the body of evidence. The highlighted statement and rationale is correct.

A SSRIs are safer as a common form of suicide was to overdose on toxic antidepressants.

This is an incorrect answer as it is only part of the argument put forward in the passage and therefore would be a poor conclusion.

B Using alternative medicine such as St John's Wort is preferable to SSRIs.

This is an incorrect answer as alternative medicines are not mentioned in the passage. One could draw this conclusion based on one's own views but it would not be supported by the content of the passage.

C More extensive research needs to be undertaken by all concerned to extend the understanding of how antidepressants and depression affect the brain.

This is the correct answer as it is the most logical conclusion that could be drawn given the information in the passage. The passage highlights the problematic nature of antidepressants and the lack of understanding all concerned have about their effects.

D   The drugs used to treat depression are no better than placebos and should not be prescribed as freely as they are.

This is an incorrect answer as the use of placebos is not discussed in the passage. Again, one could draw this conclusion based on one's own views but it would not be supported by the content of the passage.

E   The use of 'talking therapies' to treat depression would be more effective and safer than conventional drugs such as SSRIs.

This is an incorrect answer as 'talking therapies' are not detailed in the passage. This conclusion could be drawn from information acquired from other reading but it would not be supported by the content of the passage.

27   The following table shows two sets of results for a range of aptitude tests taken by a group of males and females over a period of one year (all the tests are the raw scores out of 100).

	Males 1st result	Females 1st result	Males 2nd result	Females 2nd result
Verbal	76	80	78	82
Numerical	80	78	81	81
Abstract	65	66	67	67
Mechanical	77	61	78	62
Spatial	71	69	72	70
Checking	68	77	69	78

In relation to the two sets of results which ONE of the following options is correct?

(NB: the ratios shown have been rounded to the nearest whole number)

A   *Mechanical aptitude test* – ratio of 3.5:4 males to females
Checking aptitude test – ratio of 4:3 males to females
4:3 is the largest ratio difference

B   *Mechanical aptitude test* – ratio of 4:3 males to females
Checking aptitude test – ratio of 3.5:4 males to females
4:3 is the largest ratio difference

C   *Mechanical aptitude test* – ratio of 8:6 males to females
Checking aptitude test – ratio of 7:8 males to females
7:8 is the largest ratio difference

D *Mechanical aptitude test* – ratio of 4:3 males to females
Checking aptitude test – ratio of 3:5 males to females
The ratio difference is the same

E *Mechanical aptitude test* – ratio of 3.5:3 males to females
Checking aptitude test – ratio of 3:3.5 males to females
3.5:3 is the largest ratio difference

Question 27: *answer and rationale*

Ratio: rule

This question requires you to compare two results in the form of a ratio (rounded, i.e. less than .5 round down, .5 or greater round up), identifying the greatest for both sets of results and which of the two is the largest ratio difference.

The highlighted statement and rationale is correct.

A *Mechanical aptitude test* – ratio of 3.5:4 males to females
Checking aptitude test – ratio of 4:3 males to females
4:3 is the largest ratio difference

This answer is incorrect as the ratio for Mechanical is 4:3 and for Checking 3.5:4.

B *Mechanical aptitude test* – ratio of 4:3 males to females
Checking aptitude test – ratio of 3.5:4 males to females
4:3 is the largest ratio difference

This is the correct answer.

Step 1: Calculate the rounded ratios: Mechanical – males 77 and 78, females 61 and 62, therefore both are approximately 8:6 cancelled down to 4:3; Checking – males 68 and 69, females 77 and 78, therefore both are approximately 7:8 cancelled down to 3.5:4

Step 2: Calculate the largest ratio difference between the two: 4:3 is a difference of 1 whilst 3.5:4 is only a difference of 0.5.

C *Mechanical aptitude test* – ratio of 8:6 males to females
Checking aptitude test – ratio of 7:8 males to females
7:8 is the largest ratio difference

This answer is incorrect as the ratios have not been cancelled down and 8:6 is still a larger difference than 7:8.

D *Mechanical aptitude test* – ratio of 4:3 males to females
Checking aptitude test – ratio of 3:5 males to females
The ratio difference is the same

This answer is incorrect as the ratio difference is not the same.

E   *Mechanical aptitude test* – ratio of 3.5:3 males to females
     Checking aptitude test – ratio of 3:3.5 males to females
     3.5:3 is the largest ratio difference

This answer is incorrect as all the values have been rounded down and not regarded the '.5 rule' (below .5 round down and .5 or greater round up).

28   This question relates to the passage on page 48.

     Which of the sentences in the paper is a statement of principle?

     A   'There are questions about the answerability of universities when there are complaints . . .'

     B   '. . . complaints . . . of academic inadequacy or neglect . . . cannot effectively be pursued by the vice-chancellor . . .'

     C   'But universities, though dependent on public funds, are privileged institutions with a very significant degree of self-government.'

     D   '. . . they should take complaints seriously and be seen to do so.'

     E   'The Government is concerned about the present apparent lack of account-ability . . .'

Question 28: *answer and rationale*

This question requires that you identify **the principle** in the form of a standard or rule of conduct or a set of such moral rules. The principle will usually be in the form of a general recommendation reproduced in the correct statement. The highlighted statement and rationale is correct.

A   'There are questions about the answerability of universities when there are complaints . . .'

This is an incorrect answer as essentially the sentence is purely a statement of fact that there are questions about the answerability of universities when there are complaints by students etc.

B   '. . . complaints . . . of academic inadequacy or neglect . . . cannot effectively be pursued by the vice-chancellor . . .'

This is an incorrect answer as again it is a statement of fact about the self-governing power of universities and where complaints are dealt with.

C   'But universities, though dependent on public funds, are privileged institutions with a very significant degree of self-government.'

This is an incorrect answer as this is in opposition to sentence two since it also acknowledges the universities' powers of self-regulation.

D '... they should take complaints seriously and be seen to do so.'

This is the correct answer as the sentence is a statement of principle, a standard or rule of conduct, which suggests that the principle is being neglected.

E 'The Government is concerned about the present apparent lack of accountability . . .'

This is an incorrect answer as it simply expresses the government's concern about the apparent lack of accountability and intends to discuss this with the Committee of Vice-Chancellors and Principals.

29 The following table details the carriage charges in pounds and pence for some of the services provided by Ontrack Couriers for UK mainland deliveries.

ITEM	WEIGHT	SAME DAY	NEXT DAY	3 DAYS	1 WEEK
Letter	0–100 g	1.00	0.75	–	–
Package	0–1 kg	9.95	6.95	5.95	3.95
	Up to 5 kg	11.95	8.95	7.95	5.95
	Up to 10 kg	13.95	11.95	9.95	7.95
	Up to 25 kg	15.95	13.95	11.95	9.95
	Up to 50 kg	21.99	19.99	17.99	15.95
	Up to 100 kg	47.99	40.99	33.95	30.99

A business that receives a special rate which is discounted by 20%, on packages only, wishes to send the following: 50 letters same day, 100 letters next day, 10 packages weighing 4 kg each 3-day delivery, 15 packages weighing 19 kg each same day, 3 packages weighing 49 kg 1-week delivery and 2 packages weighing 83 kg 3-day delivery.

What will be the total cost?

A £492.00

B £144.40

C £347.60

D £448.55

E £405.10

Question 29: *answer and rationale*

Percentages and multi-stage calculations: rule

This question requires the calculation of percentages, multiplication and addition.

The highlighted statement and rationale is correct.

A   £492.00

This answer is incorrect as it has not included the 20% discount on the packages.

B   £144.40

This answer is incorrect as it has added the cost of the letters with 20% of the package costs which is the discount given not the actual cost.

C   £347.60

This answer is incorrect as the cost of the letters has not been included.

D   £448.55

This answer is incorrect as the discount deducted from the packages is only 10% instead of 20%.

E   £472.60

This is the correct answer.

Step 1: Calculate the cost of the letters: letters same day $50 \times £1 = £50$ and letters next day $100 \times 75p = £75$, therefore total cost of letters = £125.

Step 2: Calculate the cost of the packages: 4 kg packages (up to 5 kg) 3-day delivery $10 \times £7.95 = £79.50$; 19 kg packages (up to 25 kg) same day delivery $15 \times £15.95 = £239.25$; 49 kg packages (up to 50 kg) 1-week delivery $3 \times £15.95 = £47.85$; 83 kg packages (up to 100 kg) 3-day delivery $2 \times £33.95 = £67.90$.

Step 3: Add the cost of the packages: £79.50 + £239.25 + £47.85 + £67.90 = £434.50.

Step 4: Calculate and deduct the 20% discount from the packages only, in other words find 80% of the total: $£434.50 \times \frac{80}{100} = £347.60$.

Step 5: Add the cost of the letters and discounted packages: £125 + £347.60 = £472.60.

30 This question relates to the passage on page 49.

Which one of the following statements best highlights the flaw in this argument?

A   The assumption is made that he has no coping strategies for such situations.

B   The assumption is that introverts cannot succeed in sales.

C   Other factors from the recruitment process are not considered.

D   It assumes that the personality test is predictive of behaviour.

E   It assumes that sales directors need to be socially bold.

Question 30: *answer and rationale*

This question requires that you can identify the **flaw** in the argument presented in the passage. This is an evaluation as to whether or not the options provided best describe the flaw in the argument, in other words are they true or false in relation to the question. In order to address this question it will be necessary to read the passage thoroughly in order to reach a conclusion as to which option would constitute the main flaw in the argument. The options may all appear feasible but you must decide which one option would question the whole premise. The highlighted statement and rationale is correct.

A   The assumption is made that he has no coping strategies for such situations.

This answer is incorrect. Whilst this option may be feasible it is not the best example of the flaw in the argument.

B   The assumption is that introverts cannot succeed in sales.

This answer is incorrect as it would require a knowledge of the differing traits between extroverts and introverts in order to arrive at this answer.

C   Other factors from the recruitment process are not considered.

This answer is incorrect. Whilst this option may be feasible it is not the best example of the flaw in the argument.

D   It assumes that the personality test is predictive of behaviour.

This is the correct answer as the assumption is made that the personality test used in the recruitment process is predictive of sales performance. As stated in the passage the test provided differing indicators for the candidate with the best sales management record and may not therefore be a valid predictor.

E   It assumes that sales directors need to be socially bold.

This answer is incorrect as it is only one of the issues raised from the personality test which relate to the flaw in the argument.

31 Getaway airport is surrounded by several tall radio masts with warning lights. The lights on the highest masts flash red every 2½ minutes, the medium masts flash blue every 4½ minutes and the lowest masts flash orange every 6 minutes. Periodically they all flash at the same time.

What is the shortest length of the interval between synchronised flashes?

A   90 minutes

B   13 minutes

C   180 minutes

D   30 minutes

E   10 minutes

Question 31: *answer and rationale*

Division: *rule*

This question contains division.

The highlighted statement and rationale is correct.

A   90 minutes

This answer is correct.

The intervals between flashes have to divide equally into the lowest possible number of minutes to arrive at synchronisation, 90 ÷ 2½ minutes = 36 times, 90 ÷ 4½ minutes = 20 times, 90 ÷ 6 minutes = 15 times, therefore 90 minutes is the shortest possible length of time.

B   13 minutes

This answer is incorrect as it cannot be evenly divided by any of the intervals in the question.

C   180 minutes

This answer is incorrect as it is not the shortest interval of time between synchronised flashes.

D   30 minutes

This answer is incorrect as the blue mast which flashes every 4½ minutes would not be synchronised with the other two.

E   10 minutes

This answer is incorrect and can be dismissed immediately as it cannot be divided by two of the intervals.

32 This question relates to the passage on page 50.

Which one of the following scenarios most closely parallels the reasoning of the above argument?

A Jennifer really wants to be a very successful actress and has dreams of winning an Oscar. She has just enrolled with RADA and will soon be on her way to her ambition.

B If you want to be very successful in finance you have to gain experience with large city firms. I do not wish to leave our small town and will have to lower my aims.

C The marriage guidance counsellor is hoping she will be able to reunite the estranged couple. They both really want this and she will talk to both of them at the next session.

D Steven really wants to achieve a first in his geology degree and has to work very hard on his assignments, projects and exam revision. He is confident that his hard work will pay dividends.

E Billy knows that to expand his building business he needs new skills such as plumbing. He has enrolled on an NVQ course in plumbing and will soon be installing bathrooms.

Question 32: *answer and rationale*

This question requires that you can examine the passage and identify a similarity in the structure or pattern of the argument that is reproduced in the correct statement. The highlighted statement and rationale is correct.

A Jennifer really wants to be a very successful actress and has dreams of winning an Oscar. She has just enrolled with RADA and will soon be on her way to her ambition.

This answer is incorrect as it is based on ideological dreams of success and does not parallel the argument of hard work, etc.

B If you want to be very successful in finance you have to gain experience with large city firms. I do not wish to leave our small town and will have to lower my aims.

This answer is incorrect and if anything is contrary to the argument put forward in the passage.

C The marriage guidance counsellor is hoping she will be able to reunite the estranged couple. They both really want this and she will talk to both of them at the next session.

This answer is incorrect as the hope of success is related to third parties and does not therefore parallel the argument in the passage.

> **D**   Steven really wants to achieve a first in his geology degree and has to work very hard on his assignments, projects and exam revision. He is confident that his hard work will pay dividends.

This answer is correct as it most closely parallels the argument in the passage. The general premise is one of hard work, determination and confidence of personal success.

E   Billy knows that to expand his building business he needs new skills such as plumbing. He has enrolled on an NVQ course in plumbing and will soon be installing bathrooms.

This answer is incorrect as there is no mention of working hard to achieve the stated goals.

33   The table below shows the daily mileage for the Easy Travel Coach Company.

	Mon	Tue	Wed	Thu	Fri	Sat	Sun
Mileage	2,000	4,000	1,500	2,000	7,250	8,750	5,900

The MD of the company wants the IT office to plot the mileage on a bar chart. The IT office allocates the task to a new member of staff who forgets to insert the detail on each axis and also enters the mileage in a different order.

Which one of the following bar charts is representative of the data?

A

B

C

D

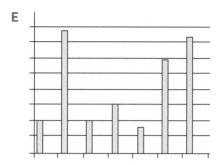

Question 33: *answer and rationale*

Interpreting data from charts: rule

This question requires that you can logically interpret data presented in bar charts where values are missing.

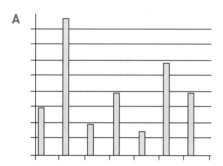

This answer is incorrect as the two values of 2,000 would have to be on an interval scale of 500 to be correct and this would result in a possible maximum of 4,500 on this chart which is too low.

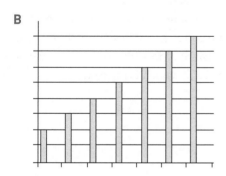

This answer is incorrect and can be dismissed immediately as it does not contain two values the same.

C

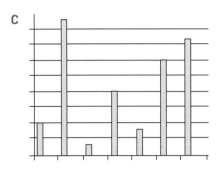

This answer is incorrect and can be dismissed immediately as it does not contain two values the same.

D

This answer is correct.

Step 1: examine the data table to find the minimum and maximum values, 1,500 and 8,750, in order to work out the interval value on the y axis. The value for this data indicates an interval value of 1,000.

Step 2: there are two values the same in the data table, so therefore check that the chart contains two values of 2,000.

Step 3: check the remaining values.

E

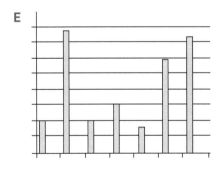

This answer is incorrect but would need to be examined carefully before dismissing it. If the two values of 2,000 are correctly displayed then the maximum possible on this chart would be 7,750 which is too low.

34 This question relates to the passage on page 52.

Which one of the following is the best conclusion that can be drawn from the extract?

A Children will see their internet speeds downgraded.

B 14% of the public support central censorship for children.

C Prohibiting people access to child pornography is an infringement of their human rights.

D Censorship is legitimate to protect children from harm.

E Filtering technology can never block children accessing unsafe pages.

Question 34: *answer and rationale*

This question requires that you can identify the **conclusion** of the argument presented in the passage. This is an evaluation as to whether the options provided are the conclusion or not, in other words are they true or false in relation to the question. In order to address this question it will be necessary to read the passage thoroughly in order to follow the ideas and structure of the argument to reach the main conclusion. The passage may contain several points that are pertinent to the overall argument as they help to build up the body of evidence. The highlighted statement and rationale is correct.

A Children will see their internet speeds downgraded.

This is the correct answer as the passage states 'A previous trial with ISP content filtering technology had the effect of reducing internet speeds (up to 86%) . . .'

B 14% of the public support central censorship for children.

This is an incorrect answer as although the passage states 'A recent poll showed 86% of the public were against internet censorship . . .' it cannot be assumed that the remaining 14% supported internet censorship, for example, some may have had no opinion on the matter – the 'don't knows'.

C Prohibiting people access to child pornography is an infringement of their human rights.

This is an incorrect answer as (a) the passage deals with the access of children to pornographic or unsafe pages, and (b) 'child pornography' is not specifically mentioned in the passage.

D   Censorship is legitimate to protect children from harm.

This is an incorrect answer as although censorship may well be a legitimate way of protecting children from harm there are issues around civil liberties and internet censorship in general.

E   Filtering technology can never block children accessing unsafe pages.

This is an incorrect answer as although the passage states 'A previous trial with ISP content filtering technology had the effect of . . . letting unsafe pages through (up to 13%)', future filtering technology may in fact let no unsafe pages through. One can never say 'never' as per the statement.

35   The park and ride bus runs Monday to Thursday from 7.30 am to 5.30 pm and from 8.30 am to 6.30 pm on Friday to Sunday. There is no break in this service and each journey lasts 8 minutes. Each bus waits 6 minutes for passengers and at very busy times the wait can be as little as 4 minutes.

In any one day what is the maximum possible number of bus journeys?

A   40

B   50

C   55

D   60

E   75

Question 35: answer and rationale

Multi-stage calculations: rule
This question contains addition, division and multiplication.

The highlighted statement and rationale is correct.

A   40

This answer is incorrect and could not be arrived at even if the longer wait time of 6 minutes were used.

B   50

This answer is correct.

Step 1: calculate the maximum possible hours in any one day: 7.30am to 5.30 pm = 10 hours, 8.30 am to 6.30 pm = 10 hours.

Step 2: calculate the maximum possible journeys per hour: each journey lasts 8 minutes and the wait can be as little as 4 minutes, therefore 8 minutes + 4 minutes = 12 minutes, 60 minutes divided by 12 minutes = 5 journeys per hour.

Step 3: calculate the maximum possible journeys in any one day (which will include busy times), 10 × 5 = 50.

C   55

This answer is incorrect and would indicate a miscalculation.

D   60

This answer is incorrect and would indicate a miscalculation.

E   75

This answer is incorrect and could only be arrived at if the wait time was not added in.

36 This question relates to the passage on page 52.

Which one of the following statements best expresses the main conclusion of the above argument?

A   5.75% of biofuels used in petrol and diesel will significantly reduce global warming.

B   Using too much land and crops for biofuels will result in food shortages.

C   Biofuels may not necessarily help tackle global warming.

D   Alternative crop production methods are necessary to reduce carbon emissions.

E   The carbon use reduction targets on all countries is obligatory.

Question 36: answer and rationale

This question requires that you can identify the **main conclusion** of the argument presented in the passage. This is an evaluation as to whether the options provided are the main conclusion, in other words are they true or false in relation to the question. In order to address this question it will be necessary to read the passage thoroughly in order to follow the ideas and structure of the argument to reach the main conclusion. The passage may contain several points that are pertinent to the overall argument as they help to build up the body of evidence. The highlighted statement and rationale is correct.

A   5.75% of biofuels used in petrol and diesel will significantly reduce global warming.

This answer is incorrect as it is only part of the argument put forward in the passage and cannot therefore be the main conclusion.

B   Using too much land and crops for biofuels will result in food shortages.

This answer is incorrect. The passage states that crops used for feeding people will be needed for the production of biofuels but this does not suggest that there will be food shortages. Overall it would be a poor conclusion to draw from this passage.

C   Biofuels may not necessarily help tackle global warming.

This is the correct answer as the passage puts forward the arguments on both sides of the debate about the use of biofuels and global warming. Which indicates that the negatives may equal the positives in terms of pollution and energy use.

D   Alternative crop production methods are necessary to reduce carbon emissions.

This answer is incorrect as alternative methods of crop production are not discussed in the passage. One could conclude that this potentially could be the answer to the problem of biofuel production but it would not be the best conclusion of the information available.

E   The carbon use reduction targets on all countries is obligatory.

This answer is incorrect and is not supported by the information in the passage and is therefore irrelevant to the argument.

37 A round box of chocolates with a diameter of 40 cm and a depth of 3 cm is gift wrapped and tied with a 250 cm length of ribbon which is tied in a bow on top as shown below. After completion of the gift wrapping 60 cm of ribbon was left.

Bottom   Side   Top

A second piece of ribbon also measuring 250 cm is used to decorate a second gift. The ribbon is tied in a similar bow to the first gift and all the ribbon is used.

How many boxes of chocolates are there in the second gift?

A   6

B   10

C   5

D   4

E   12

Question 37: *answer and rationale*

Extracting relevant information and multi-stage calculations: rule

This question contains addition, multiplication and division.

The highlighted statement and rationale is correct.

A   6

This answer is correct.

Step 1: the question contains information that is irrelevant to the calculation; to answer the question the only relevant measures are the depth of the box (3 cm) and the amount of extra ribbon available for use (60 cm).

Step 2: from the diagrams it can be seen that the ribbon crosses the depth of the box four times, therefore 3 cm $\times$ 4 = 12 cm, therefore each additional box will use up 12 cm more of the ribbon.

Step 3: calculate the number of additional boxes of chocolates: 60 cm of extra ribbon divided by 12 cm required for each box = 5, add this to the original box = 6.

B   10

This answer is incorrect and would indicate a miscalculation.

C   5

This answer is incorrect and would equal the additional boxes only.

D   4

This answer is incorrect and would indicate a miscalculation.

E   12

This answer is incorrect and would indicate that the depth of the box has only been counted twice instead of four times.

38 This question relates to the passage on page 53.

Which one of the following is the best statement of the flaw in the above argument?

A It does not take into account the profound effect the weather can have on the tide.

B It ignores the fact that some areas only have one tide.

C The assumption made is one of cause and effect.

D It overlooks spring tides when the lunar and solar tides line up.

E It ignores the fact that strong winds and abnormal atmospheric pressure makes it impossible to predict tide levels.

Question 38: *answer and rationale*

This question requires that you can identify the **flaw** in the argument presented in the passage. This is an evaluation as to whether the options provided best describe the flaw in the argument, in other words are they true or false in relation to the question. In order to address this question it will be necessary to read the passage thoroughly in order to reach a conclusion as to which option would constitute the main flaw in the argument. The options may all appear feasible but you must decide which one option would question the whole premise. The highlighted statement and rationale is correct.

A It does not take into account the profound effect the weather can have on the tide.

This answer is incorrect on the basis of the information available in the passage. That is not to say that the statement itself is inaccurate.

B It ignores the fact that some areas only have one tide.

This answer is incorrect and is irrelevant in terms of the question being asked.

C The assumption made is one of cause and effect.

This is the correct answer as the assumption being made is that the level of the alternating tides is created by the gravitational pull of the moon on the earth which is basically cause and effect.

D It overlooks spring tides when the lunar and solar tides line up.

This answer is incorrect as the passage does not make reference to spring tides and for this statement to be correct external knowledge would have to be applied.

E It ignores the fact that strong winds and abnormal atmospheric pressure makes it impossible to predict tide levels.

This answer is incorrect and could not be arrived at without applying further information.

39 A game has two bags of balls. Bag 'A' contains four red balls and four blue balls. Bag 'B' contains four red bats and four blue bats.

To play a game you have to have a matching red bat and red ball which are drawn from the bags whilst blindfolded. To achieve this, what is the *least* number of bats and balls you must draw from the bags?

A Five balls and one bat.

B Three balls and three bats.

C Four balls and four bats.

D Five balls and four bats.

E Five balls and five bats.

Question 39: *answer and rationale*

Dependent events and random: rule

This question is based on dependent events, in other words, the probabilities of the second event will be influenced by the outcomes of the first event and so on. However, random events will also influence the outcome and this random effect has to be eliminated.

The highlighted statement and rationale is correct.

A Five balls and one bat.

This answer is incorrect. It is certain that you would have a matching bat and ball but they could be either blue or red and therefore the outcome is not certain.

B Three balls and three bats.

This answer is incorrect and it would depend on the luck of the draw which could result in a red bat and ball but might not and therefore the outcome is not certain.

C Four balls and four bats.

This answer is incorrect and it would depend on the luck of the draw which could result in a red bat and ball but might not and therefore the outcome is not certain.

D Five balls and four bats.

This answer is incorrect as the blindfolded draw of the bat could result in four blue bats being drawn.

E   Five balls and five bats.

This answer is correct.

Step 1: if the first ball drawn from Bag 'A' is blue then the probability of drawing a red ball is increased, and so on, but as the balls are being drawn at random then there is always a possibility that four blue balls will be drawn before a red one or vice versa. Therefore, five balls must be drawn to ensure the draw of a red ball.

Step 2: the draw for a bat will be dependent on the same principle as the draw for the balls and the first four bats drawn could be blue, therefore you will still have to draw five bats to ensure having a red bat.

40   This question relates to the passage on page 54.

Which one of the following statements could be implied from this passage?

A   The UK should adopt the US system of having nine Justices.

B   Justices' decisions should ideally be based on a majority of their total number.

C   Decisions of the Justices would be improved by a US-style system.

D   Appeal decisions will always be influenced by the identity of the Justices on the panel.

E   In the UK decisions in appeals are decided by a panel of five Justices.

Question 40: *answer and rationale*

To be **implied** means something that can be suggested but not overtly expressed; the act of reading between the lines or otherwise understanding a message that is implicit. You need to read the passage carefully to identify the overall argument and determine which one option best answers the question posed. The highlighted statement and rationale is correct.

A   The UK should adopt the US system of having nine Justices.

This is an incorrect answer as there is nothing in the passage that suggests or implies the UK should have nine Justices instead of the current twelve, although such a move would in fact answer the criticism raised by the passage.

B   Justices' decisions should ideally be based on a majority of their total number.

This is the correct answer as the passage actually states that there should be 'an increase in the number of Justices hearing appeals; with at the very least a majority of the total involved in important cases'.

C Decisions of the Justices would be improved by a US-style system.

This is an incorrect answer as although 'The UK system is currently seen by many as a lottery and . . . the outcome may also be dependent on the identity of the individual Justices involved', it cannot be determined from this subjective statement that the decisions of the Justices would be improved by a US-style system without further information.

D Appeal decisions will always be influenced by the identity of the Justices on the panel.

This is an incorrect answer. The passage states 'The UK system is currently seen by many as a lottery and . . . the outcome may also be dependent on the identity of the individual Justices involved.' The 'outcome may' does not mean that the decisions will 'always' be influenced by the identity of the Justices on the panel.

E In the UK decisions in appeals are decided by a panel of five Justices.

This is an incorrect answer as the passage states 'Apart from exceptional cases such as those of high constitutional or great public importance, the Justices almost always sit as a panel of five . . .' Justices 'almost always' so not 'always' sit as a panel of five and obviously not in 'exceptional cases'.

41 Below is a table detailing golf buggy hire.

TIGER GOLF CLUB
Summer buggy hire
7 am – 8 pm, 7 days per week

HOURLY RATE	
7 am – 5 pm	£3.50 per hour
5 pm – 8 pm	£2.25 per hour
½ day hire 7 am – 1 pm	£16.00
All day hire	£20.00
Refundable deposit £20.00	

How much will it cost to hire a golf buggy from 2 pm for 5 hours?

A £17.50

B £16.00

C £15.00

D   £20.00

E   £11.25

Question 41: answer and rationale

Extracting information and multi-stage calculations: rule

This question requires that you can extract the relevant information and perform multiplication and addition.

The highlighted statement and rationale is correct.

A   £17.50

This answer is incorrect as it would be the result of 5 hours at £3.50 and 2 hours of the required hire time are at the lesser rate of £2.25.

B   £16.00

This answer is incorrect as it is the ½ day hire rate of £16 between 7 am and 1 pm which is too early for the required hire time.

C   £15.00

This answer is correct.

Step 1: extract the relevant information: buggy hire from 2 pm for 5 hours, 2 pm to 5 pm = 3 hours × £3.50 = £10.50, 5 pm to 7 pm = 2 hours × £2.25 = £4.50.

Step 2: add hire rates: £10.50 + £4.50 = £15 (note the refundable deposit is redundant information as it is not an actual cost).

D   £20.00

This answer is incorrect as it is the rate for a full day hire which would exceed the rate for 5 hours.

E   £11.25

This answer is incorrect as it is the rate for 5 hours commencing at 5 pm which is too late for the required hire.

42 This question relates to the passage on page 55.

Which one of the following statements can be concluded from this report?

A   The death rate of company directors and lawyers in the North East is the same as their colleagues in the South East.

B   Socio-economic groups may only be one of the factors affecting higher
     mortality rates in the North East.

C   The death rate of professional people in the North East is higher than for
     managers in the South East.

D   Female cleaners in the North East and South East have lower death rates than
     men in the same areas.

E   Male lawyers working in London have a higher death rate than their colleagues
     in the North East.

Question 42: answer and rationale

This question requires that you can identify the **conclusion** of the argument presented in
the passage. This is an evaluation as to whether the options provided are the conclusion or
not, in other words are they true or false in relation to the question. In order to address this
question it will be necessary to read the passage thoroughly in order to follow the ideas
and structure of the argument to reach the main conclusion. The passage may contain
several points that are pertinent to the overall argument as they help to build up the body
of evidence. The highlighted statement and rationale is correct.

A   The death rate of company directors and lawyers in the North East is the same as
     their colleagues in the South East.

This answer is incorrect as the passage clearly states that 'Men in higher managerial and
professional occupations – such as company directors and lawyers – in the South East
(excluding London) had the lowest rate, at 179 per 100,000.'

B   Socio-economic groups may only be one of the factors affecting higher mortality
     rates in the North East.

This is an incorrect answer as although socio-economic groups may only be one of the
factors in relation to death rates, and although it may appear obvious, there is no
indication of this in the passage.

C   The death rate of professional people in the North East is higher than for
     managers in the South East.

This is the correct answer as the passage clearly states that men in higher managerial and
professional occupations in the South East had the lowest death rate of any of the socio-
economic groups.

D Female cleaners in the North East and South East have lower death rates than men in the same areas.

This is an incorrect answer as the passage only relates to research undertaken on the working male population.

E Male lawyers working in London have a higher death rate than their colleagues in the North East.

This is an incorrect answer as, although this may be the case, the passage relates specifically to the South East (excluding London) and so any comparison of death rates cannot be made.

43 June is helping her dad pack bait for his pest control business. The bait is in 10 g packets. June asks her dad how many packets of bait he needs. Her dad informs her that he sets 20 traps and places 20 g of bait in each trap. He works an 8 hour day and he checks all the traps every hour. During the first 5 hours he has to add 10 g of bait to half the traps each hour. During the last 3 hours he has to add 5 g of bait to three-quarters of the traps. If there is a part packet left he adds it to the last trap.

How many packets of bait does June need to pack for her dad?

A 58

B 37.5

C 38

D 57.5

E 60

Question 43: *answer and rationale*

Multi-stage calculation: rule
This question requires that you can perform multiplication, division and addition.

The highlighted statement and rationale is correct.

A 58

This answer is correct.

Step 1: 1 packet = 10 g, 20 traps × 20 g (2 packets) = 40 packets.

Step 2: 10 g (1 packet) is added to half the traps during the first 5 hours, 20 ÷ 2 = 10 traps × 10 g (1 packet) = 10 packets.

Step 3: 5 g (½ packet) is added to three quarters of the traps during the last 3 hours, 20 ÷ 4 × 3 = 15 traps × 5 g (½ packet) = 7½ packets.

Step 4: remaining ½ packet is added to last trap, therefore total = 40 + 10 + 7½ + ½ = 58

B   37.5

This answer is incorrect as it would not be sufficient to set the 20 g in each of the 20 traps at the start of the day and can be dismissed immediately.

C   38

This answer is incorrect as it would not be sufficient to set the 20 g in each of the 20 traps at the start of the day and can be dismissed immediately.

D   57.5

This answer is incorrect as the remaining part packet (½), has not been added.

E   60

This answer is incorrect as you are not being asked to round up to the nearest ten.

44 This question relates to the passage on page 56.

Which one of the following statements, if true, would detract from the above argument?

A   The number of people contracting STDs will decrease in the future.

B   Providing educational resources for health management is expensive.

C   National Health Service Trusts have increased expenditure on STD educational programmes at the same level as AIDS programmes.

D   The social stigma attached to people who contract STDs will diminish over time.

E   Further scientific advances will reduce the medical interventions required for people with STDs.

Question 44: *answer and rationale*

This question requires that you can identify which statement, **if factual**, would detract from the power of the argument presented in the passage. This is an evaluation as to whether the options provided, if they were true, would most weaken the argument. In order to address this question it will be necessary to read the passage thoroughly in order to arrive at the most logical answer. The options may all appear feasible but you must decide which one option would be the most likely. The highlighted statement and rationale is correct.

A   The number of people contracting STDs will decrease in the future.

This is the correct answer given the content of the passage and the statistical fact that the spread of STDs has increased year on year since accurate records were first kept; it would be true that a decrease in the numbers would contradict the argument.

B   Providing educational resources for health management is expensive.

This answer is incorrect as the costs of health management are probably the main reason for the lack of educational programmes designed to reduce or eliminate STDs and if this statement were true then it would support the argument and not detract from it.

C   National Health Service Trusts have increased expenditure on STD educational programmes at the same level as AIDS programmes.

This answer is incorrect as the passage indicates that the expenditure on STD educational programmes is less and even if it were true then it would support rather than detract from the argument.

D   The social stigma attached to people who contract STDs will diminish over time.

This answer is incorrect as the claim that the social stigma attached to STDs has lessened and that it will diminish further over time forms part of the argument as to why there is a lack of adequate educational resources to reduce or eliminate them.

E   Further scientific advances will reduce the medical interventions required for people with STDs.

This answer is incorrect because if this were true then this would give substance to the view that the obligations to educational programmes are not as great as they were.

45   A cube has sides that each measure 40 cm in length.

What is the volume of the cube?

A   0.064 m

B   0.064 m^2

C   0.16 m^2

D   64,000 cm^3

E   1,600 cm^2

Question 45: *answer and rationale*

Volume: rule

To find the volume of a cuboid multiply the length by the width by the height.

The highlighted statement and rationale is correct.

A   0.064 m

This answer is incorrect as it has the incorrect units of m instead of cm^3.

B   0.064 m^2

This answer is incorrect as it has the incorrect units m^2 instead of cm^3.

C   0.16 m^2

This answer is incorrect as it has the incorrect units m^2 instead of cm^3.

D   64,000 cm^3

This is the correct answer.

Step 1: the length of each side is 40 cm therefore the volume is $40 \times 40 \times 40 = 64,000$ cm^3. This answer is also the only option that has the correct units, namely cm^3.

E   1,600 cm^2

This answer is incorrect as it is the area of one side of the cube and therefore it has the incorrect units of cm^2 instead of cm^3.

46 This question relates to the passage on page 57.

Which one of the following statements most closely mirrors the reasoning of the above argument?

A   If the present level of storm and flood damage does not end soon then insurance companies will be inundated with claims. Some insurance companies may struggle to meet the level of claims and payments could take some time. If storm and flood damage become a feature of our climate insurance companies may add extra clauses to policies.

B   If the cost of fuel continues to rise, then people will be more economical and will buy less fuel. The fuel prices will then stop increasing if less fuel is purchased. Therefore, the rise in fuel prices must peak soon.

C　If we do not pay our skilled workers more, many of them will seek work abroad. We will then be left with a national skills shortage. Therefore, wages for skilled workers must increase if we wish to maintain a high skills base in this country.

D　If we are all prepared to pay more road tax, then the government could afford to improve the road network. An improved road network would result in shorter more cost effective transport. Therefore, if we want a more efficient road system, we must be prepared to pay higher road tax.

E　The UK car industry has been downsizing for some time. If the industry continues to decrease job losses will be high. Towns and cities whose economies depend on the salaries of car workers would suffer as a consequence. If the decline in the car industry continues then these towns and cities will be badly affected.

Question 46: answer and rationale

This question requires that you can examine the passage and identify a similarity in the structure or pattern of the argument that is reproduced in the correct statement. The highlighted statement and rationale is correct.

A　If the present level of storm and flood damage does not end soon then insurance companies will be inundated with claims. Some insurance companies may struggle to meet the level of claims and payments could take some time. If storm and flood damage become a feature of our climate insurance companies may add extra clauses to policies.

This answer is incorrect as the economic impact highlighted in this statement is due to what could be termed 'acts of god' or naturally occurring problems which are outside the realms of control.

B　If the cost of fuel continues to rise, then people will be more economical and will buy less fuel. The fuel prices will then stop increasing if less fuel is purchased. Therefore, the rise in fuel prices must peak soon.

This answer is incorrect as it is more a statement about the economies of supply and demand.

C　If we do not pay our skilled workers more, many of them will seek work abroad. We will then be left with a national skills shortage. Therefore, wages for skilled workers must increase if we wish to maintain a high skills base in this country.

This answer is incorrect as again it is related to a supply and demand situation.

D　If we are all prepared to pay more road tax, then the government could afford to improve the road network. An improved road network would result in shorter more cost effective transport. Therefore, if we want a more efficient road system, we must be prepared to pay higher road tax.

This answer is incorrect as it relates to paying more for an improved service which is a completely different economic argument to the one in the passage.

E   The UK car industry has been downsizing for some time. If the industry continues to decrease job losses will be high. Towns and cities whose economies depend on the salaries of car workers would suffer as a consequence. If the decline in the car industry continues then these towns and cities will be badly affected.

This is the correct answer as it most closely mirrors the economic argument in the passage caused by recession.

47 Jane buys biscuits once a fortnight for her grandmother. Her grandmother's favourite biscuits are 96p per packet and she gives Jane enough money for her usual fortnightly supply. At the supermarket there is a multi-buy offer on 10 packets or more. This reduces the packets by 16p each and Jane realises that her grandmother can now have two more packets of biscuits.

How many packets of biscuits does she buy?

A   10

B   12

C   14

D   16

E   20

Question 47: answer and rationale

Multi-stage calculation: rule
This question contains subtraction, multiplication and addition.

The highlighted statement and rationale is correct.

A   10

This answer is incorrect as it would equate to the number of packets of biscuits Jane could buy before the multi-buy offer.

B 12

This answer is correct.

Step 1: calculate the multi-buy offer price: 96p per packet – 16p reduction = offer price of 80p per packet.

Step 2: Jane realises she can buy her grandmother two more packets at the reduced rate, $2 \times 80p = £1.60$ which is equal $16p \times 10$, therefore Jane must have originally had enough money to buy 10 packets.

Step 3: 10 packets + 2 packets = 12 packets

C 14

This answer is incorrect and would indicate a miscalculation.

D 16

This answer is incorrect as the value 16 only relates to the 16p reduction in price.

E 20

This answer is incorrect and would indicate a gross miscalculation.

48 This question relates to the passage on page 58.

Which one of the following statements can be concluded from this extract?

A Companies need to be aware of their obligations to employees before making blanket policies.

B The customer is always right and should be able to determine whom they will deal with on a business basis.

C The government is responsible for ensuring discrimination legislation reflects companies' working practices.

D Had the Jewish clients been female then there would have been no case of sexual harassment.

E Company policies may contain procedures that allow for positive discrimination in politically sensitive situations.

Question 48: *answer and rationale*

This question requires that you can identify the **conclusion** of the argument presented in the passage. This is an evaluation as to whether the options provided are the conclusion or not, in other words are they true or false in relation to the question. In order to address this question it will be necessary to read the passage thoroughly in order to follow the ideas and structure of the argument to reach the main conclusion. The passage may contain several points that are pertinent to the overall argument as they help to build up the body of evidence. The highlighted statement and rationale is correct.

A   Companies need to be aware of their obligations to employees before making blanket policies.

This is the correct answer as from the extract it appears that the company made policies 'on the basis of race' by acquiescing to their clients perceived sensibilities, in this case that Jewish clients would prefer not to be handled by Muslim women.

B   The customer is always right and should be able to determine whom they will deal with on a business basis.

This is an incorrect answer and is ostensibly an old cliché in the world of equality and diversity and has no bearing on the extract of the case.

C   The government is responsible for ensuring discrimination legislation reflects companies' working practices.

This is an incorrect answer as it is not stated in the extract of the case. What is mentioned is that the government should be aware of problems companies have in this area when introducing future equality legislation.

D   Had the Jewish clients been female then there would have been no case of sexual harassment.

This is an incorrect answer as it is totally irrelevant to the question posed and in any event further information would be required regarding the law in relation to sexual harassment.

E   Company policies may contain procedures that allow for positive discrimination in politically sensitive situations

This is an incorrect answer as there is no mention of policies that could be made in relation to 'positive discrimination in politically sensitive situations' irrespective of the fact that in any event this would be extremely dubious.

49   I am having friends round this evening for a barbeque. Some of my friends are vegetarian and I can't cook their veggie burgers and veggie sausages with the meat ones. We are due to eat at 7.00 pm and I have drawn up a timed 'To Do' list as follows:

'TO DO' LIST

Make beef burgers and skewer sausages 15 minutes

Barbeque beef burgers and sausages 30 minutes

Cut bread rolls 10 minutes

Make salad dressing 10 minutes

Wash salad 5 minutes

Toss salad in dressing 5 minutes

Make veggie burgers and veggie sausages 30 minutes

Barbeque veggie burgers and veggie sausages 30 minutes

Put veggie food in hot store 5 minutes

Put out patio furniture and lay the table 15 minutes

My barbeque has one grill area and an area for storing hot food. I will serve the food as soon as the meat burgers and sausages are cooked.

What is the latest time I should start preparing the food?

A   5.10 pm

B   5.25 pm

C   5.30 pm

D   4.25 pm

E   5.20 pm

Question 49: answer and rationale

Extracting relevant information and basic calculation: rule

This question requires that you can extract relevant information and avoid any distracting information. Basic addition and subtraction are then required.

A   5.10 pm

This answer is incorrect as it would possibly indicate that tasks that could be carried out during cooking time have been included.

B   5.25 pm

This answer is correct.

Step 1: extract the relevant information: some friends are vegetarian, due to eat at 7.00 pm, one grill and an area for storing, serve as soon as meat burgers and sausages are cooked, what is the latest time to start preparing.

Step 2: vegetarian burgers and sausages have to be made and cooked first to avoid contamination, 30 minutes preparation + 30 minutes cooking time + 5 minutes to store when cooked = 1 hour 5 minutes.

Step 3: making the beef burgers and skewering the sausages 15 minutes + washing the salad 5 minutes + making the salad dressing 10 minutes + toss salad in dressing 5 minutes = 35 minutes, which can be carried out whilst the vegetarian option is cooking and therefore does not need to be added to the total time.

Step 4: the beef burgers and sausages take 30 minutes to barbeque and during this time the bread can be cut (10 minutes) and the patio furniture, etc. put out (15 minutes), which leaves 5 minutes spare.

Step 5: calculate total time required, 1 hour 5 minutes + 30 minutes = 1 hour 35 minutes, therefore the latest time to begin preparing the food is 7.00 pm – 1 hour 35 minutes = 5.25 pm.

C   5.30 pm

This answer is incorrect and would possibly indicate that the time required to store the vegetarian food has not been added to the total.

D   4.25 pm

This answer is incorrect and would possibly indicate that all the times from the 'To Do' list have been added into the total.

E   5.20 pm

This answer is incorrect and would indicate a possible miscalculation.

50   This question relates to the passage on page 59.

Which one of the following statements is an underlying assumption of the above argument?

A   All religions believe in reincarnation.

B   Mediums can make contact with people who are dead.

    C   Those who believe in the spirit world are often relatives of the recently bereaved.

    D   Mediums, fortune-tellers and astrologers have extra-sensory perception.

    E   Talking to dead loved ones is a comfort to surviving relations and friends.

Question 50: *answer and rationale*

An **assumption** is a proposition that is taken for granted, that is, as if it were known to be true. It is a statement that can be surmised or postulated given the overall context of the passage. This question is asking you to identify which statement can be surmised or postulated from the passage. In identifying an **assumption** the correct statement will not actually be stated in the passage so it is for you to determine the main argument and look for the reasoning to support this conclusion. You need to read the passage carefully to identify the overall argument and determine which one option best answers the question posed. The highlighted statement and rationale is correct.

A   All religions believe in reincarnation.

This is an incorrect answer as the passage refers to life after death in terms of the 'spirit world' and not reincarnation in some other life form, therefore this assumption could not be made.

B   Mediums can make contact with people who are dead.

This is an incorrect answer. The passage indicates that there are mediums who purport to communicate with those who are dead but one could not assume that this statement is true from the content of the passage.

C   Those who believe in the spirit world are often relatives of the recently bereaved.

This is an incorrect answer as the assumption cannot be made that the relations and friends referred to in the passage actually believe in the spirit world even though they make use of mediums.

D   Mediums, fortune-tellers and astrologers have extra-sensory perception.

This is an incorrect answer as the statements made in the passage about mediums, fortune-tellers and astrologers make no claims to the truth let alone alluding to the powers of extra-sensory perception.

E   Talking to dead loved ones is a comfort to surviving relations and friends.

This is the correct answer as the assumption can be made from the passage that those relations or friends who seek out mediums, etc. do take comfort from communications with the dead whatever the case may or may not be in reality for the efficacy of such liaisons. If this were not true then there would be no call for their services.

Chapter 5
TSA Writing Task

17. Introduction

The Writing Task is only used by the University of Oxford TSA and not by Cambridge.

It is as important to prepare for this part of the TSA as it is for the Thinking Skills Assessment. First, the type of questions with which you will be confronted may be very different from what you have been used to in your previous educational experiences. Second, the time constraint of 30 minutes really does focus the mind and you need to develop the skills of structure and content within this constraint.

This section is extremely relevant to your application as the Writing Task has been included by Oxford specifically to test the skills that they consider will be important for your degree programme. Your product from this task should demonstrate that you have the ability or potential ability to:

- recognise and resolve conflict
- formulate and provide valid support for logical arguments
- consider alternative explanations for difficult ideas.

Probably the most singular thing you can do to prepare for this task is to read a variety of broadsheet newspapers and keep up to date through magazines, periodicals, etc., both generally and specifically in relation to your preferred subject(s) (i.e. intended degree subjects). These 'quality' newspapers, magazines, etc. often provide conflicting views and arguments on a range of topical issues that will undoubtedly be the subject of one or more of the Writing Task questions. The more familiar you are with these views and arguments the better you should perform. Obviously, it would be preferable to get into a routine of reading broadsheet newspapers over a period of several months rather than a week or two before the assessment!

18. TSA Writing Task

The TSA Writing Task requires you to write a single short essay within 30 minutes. Normally three essay questions are provided from which you select only one. The essay questions will be on general subjects that do not require any specialised knowledge.

At the outset of the task you will be provided with a set of instructions and a separate answer booklet for your essay. Two blank pages are provided within the answer booklet that you can use for making notes before writing the essay. More information about this task can be found on the Oxford website.

Each of the three essay questions are followed by two or three statements relating directly to the question and which should be addressed in the essay.

Here are two examples of the type of question and additional statements with which you might be presented:

1. **What are the arguments for and against the introduction of proportional representation in general elections?**

    Write a unified essay to address this question, in which you consider the following:

    Who would gain and who would lose by proportional representation?

    Would minor parties have an inequitable say in the government of the country?

    Why are governments elected by proportional representation seen as ineffective?

2. **What is your response to the view that the international agreements on the emission of greenhouse gases are ineffective?**

    Write a unified essay to address this question, in which you consider the following:

    What are the competing issues of the world's superpowers in relation to controlling greenhouse gas emissions?

    Who will be the losers if the international agreements are effective?

    Who should be leading the way on climate change action?

19. *Structured approach*

It is important that each of the following stages is considered separately before you attempt writing the essay:

- Identify what is being asked in each of the questions
- Identify the question that you would be best able to answer
- Brainstorm the issues and arguments relevant to the question
- Plan the structure
- Write the essay
- Revision

You may be one of those people in the top few per cent of the population who can just write a well-reasoned essay without any preparation or planning. If you are not then time spent on the first four stages will be time well spent before you start actually writing the essay. Give yourself up to 5 MINUTES for these four stages, probably a couple of minutes for the first two stages and 3 minutes for the next stages. Control your natural urge to skip these stages to ensure you properly plan and prepare – as the old saying goes, 'failing to plan is planning to fail!'

Identifying the question

At the outset you may convince yourself that you know next to nothing about any of the essay questions on offer. DON'T PANIC! No matter what the subject there will be very few occasions where you are unable to come up with a number of relevant ideas to form a useful structure from your own knowledge and experience and invariably this is the process that is of interest to the examiners.

In your anxiety you will want to get on with writing the essay but you should resist this temptation and spend a few minutes making sure you will be answering the question being asked. The question will usually provide you with both the structure of the essay and sometimes the abilities you are required to display.

It sounds obvious, but it is important to be absolutely sure what the question is asking you to do. It has often been the case that a person reads into the question something that isn't there and so writes the whole essay without answering the question.

Let's look at the example essay topics given above and unpack them to determine what is being asked:

1. **What are the arguments for and against the introduction of proportional representation in general elections?**

    This question can be broken down easily into four constituent parts, i.e. *'What are the arguments/for and against/the introduction of proportional representation/in general elections?'*

    'What are the arguments' is essentially asking for the reasons *for and against the introduction of proportional representation.* Reasons include evidence, principles, assumptions and logical inferences or causal connections which are given to support judgements and recommendations. Further details about arguments, reasons and conclusions are provided under the heading 'Writing the essay'.

    'for and against' is asking for the pros and cons of *the introduction of proportional representation . . .* This is not asking you for your own ideas and thoughts on the issue and you need to keep focused on what is being asked.

'the introduction of proportional representation/in general elections' are both very specific and your arguments must retain a focus on these.

2.   **What is your response to the view that the international agreements on the emission of greenhouse gases are ineffective?**

This question can be broken down into five constituent parts, though the last two parts might preferably be combined, i.e. *'What is your response/to the view/that the international agreements/on the emission of greenhouse gases/are ineffective?'*

'What is your response' is asking for your reaction to the question posed. It invites you to present both evidence, principles, assumptions and logical inferences, as well as your own thoughts on the issue.

'to the view' is suggesting that there are apparently opposing views to the one given and they should be raised and considered in the essay.

'that the international agreements' is quite specific and in answering this question you would need to demonstrate a certain amount of knowledge in this area.

'on the emission of greenhouse gases' is quite specific and in answering the question you would need to demonstrate a certain amount of knowledge of the causes and impact of the emission of greenhouse gases.

'are ineffective' is making a definitive statement which should be considered in that light and contested or otherwise.

The two examples given above may appear somewhat long-winded. In reality this would not be the case. It would probably take less than a minute to identify and note down the constituent parts of any particular question to make sure your essay will directly answer the chosen question.

There may be more than one question that you feel able to answer but you need to consider which one would allow you best to demonstrate your analytical abilities. The examiners are looking for a 'well-reasoned' essay.

Some questions may lend themselves to a more 'argumentative' approach, examining the various pros and cons of the issue(s) raised and forming some kind of conclusions, for example, in relation to the 'sample essays' above, the question, *'What are the arguments for and against the introduction of proportional representation in general elections?'*

Other questions may require a more analytical or critical approach, requiring you to show you can identify more difficult abstract concepts, for example, in relation to the 'sample essays' above, the question, *'What is your response to the view that the international agreements on the emission of greenhouse gases are ineffective?'* Both types of questions will obviously influence the way in which your essay is structured and some type of structure should already be forming in your mind, even subconsciously, before you move onto the next stage.

Brainstorming the issues

There is no doubt that when universities examine essays they are looking for good analytical ability in order to distinguish between better performers. It is suggested by some academic writers that analysis and brainstorming are two separate concepts. In analysis the individual identifies and analyses the concepts and implications of the question. They then write down their own ideas identifying the concepts' essential characteristics. In the other concept the individual is simply brainstorming their own ideas. The analysis concept requires considerable time to unravel and consequently is not advised for use in essays under test conditions.

Brainstorming is coming up with a number of ideas from your own knowledge and experience and writing them down even if they are not relevant. You can easily discard the irrelevant ideas afterwards. Essentially, the product of brainstorming will provide the basis for the essay structure and the content.

There are a number of different techniques available when brainstorming: it can be totally organic and unstructured, or more structured methods such as mind-mapping and the use of mnemonics can be used. You may be familiar with or used to a particular method and if so, use it. Some people find mind-mapping beneficial, others don't. If you haven't previously used this method and it appeals to you, buy a book on it; there are plenty available. We will concentrate on the assistance to brainstorming that can be provided by mnemonics in relation to essay writing.

Children are often taught to remember the colours of the rainbow using the mnemonic, 'Richard of York gave battle in vain' – red, orange, yellow, green, blue, indigo and violet. Students would normally use mnemonics where they are learnt for specific knowledge-based examinations.

However, there are two useful mnemonics that are often used for providing a structure into which you can place your ideas and thoughts or which themselves supply a vehicle and structure for encouraging such ideas and thoughts.

The first mnemonic, often useful in answering 'argue for and against' type questions, though also used for more open questions, is referred to as a **SWOT** analysis – **S**trengths, **W**eaknesses, **O**pportunities and **T**hreats.

We will use this mnemonic in examining the example essay question, *'What are the arguments for and against the introduction of proportional representation in general elections?'*

Strengths:	May encourage people to vote
	More representative government
Weaknesses:	Hung parliaments
	Lack of leadership
	Weak government
Opportunities:	Focus on the needs of the electorate
	Policies represent the needs of the electorate
	Greater democracy
	More say in government
	Liberal Democrats manifesto
Threats:	Policies become ineffective
	Government over-representative of minority groups
	All talk and no action

The second mnemonic provides a broad 'analysis' of a question and is referred to as **PESTEL** analysis – **P**olitical, **E**conomic, **S**ocial, **T**echnical, **E**nvironmental and **L**egal.

We will use this mnemonic in examining the example essay question, *'What is your response to the view that the international agreements on the emission of greenhouse gases are ineffective?'*

Political:	Kyoto Agreement (international)
	USA not signatory
	Welfare
	Electability
Economic:	Cost benefit
	Developing countries
	Employment
	Demography
Social:	Health
	Employment
	Leisure
	Transport
Technical:	Other energy sources
Environmental:	Ozone depletion in stratosphere
	Greenhouse gases in the troposphere
	Transport
Legal:	Treaties
	Compensation
	Enforcement/sanctions

Ideas are organic in that they grow and develop over time. Consequently, at stages throughout your writing other ideas will come to you that have not been included in the structure. You may consider that some of these ideas are sufficiently important to issues or arguments you have raised that it is essential they are included. When you think of them note them on one of the blank pages provided so that you don't forget them. These additional ideas can often be inserted within the final section of the essay where you are providing a summary or synthesis of the issues or arguments.

Planning the structure

Whatever technique you have used to brainstorm your chosen question you should now have sufficient material with which to plan your structure.

The Writing Task questions provided by Oxford in fact provide the outline structure for your essay. In relation to the example question *'What is your response to the view that the international agreements on the emission of greenhouse gases are ineffective?'* you are required to consider the following three questions:

- What are the competing issues of the world's superpowers in relation to controlling greenhouse gas emissions?
- Who will be the losers if the international agreements are effective?
- Who should be leading the way on climate change action?

It therefore follows that your essay should be structured in three specific parts in order to answer these three questions.

Although it seems pretty obvious, all essays need a beginning, middle and an end, but it is surprising how often even good students forget this rule. A useful way to apply this rule is as follows:

The beginning is: **tell them what you're going to tell them.**

The opening paragraph or paragraphs gives the reader, in this case an examiner, advance notice of the overall direction and substance of your essay.

The middle is: **tell them**.

Tell them the answer to the question which, if using the mnemonic structure, would include the substance of the SWOT or PESTEL analysis.

The end is: **tell them what you've told them**.

In this part you can summarise or synthesise your arguments or analysis, that is, *'What is your response to the view that the international agreements on the emission of greenhouse gases are ineffective?'*

20. Writing the essay

The most effective way of creating a structure is by the use of paragraphs. There will be a paragraph for the introduction, separate paragraphs for each of the 'arguments' and a paragraph for the conclusion. You are not writing a short story with its discursive narrative; you are providing an analysis of the question and developing reasoned arguments.

The content of the introductory paragraph is very important. It provides the opportunity to grab the attention of the reader. The introduction will reflect how good or bad the rest of the essay is going to be and how it will be perceived by an examiner who has many more ahead of him or her! It must set the scene and give a direction as to what can be expected in the body of the essay (not in the conclusion).

In relation to paragraphing the 'arguments', where you are considering 'arguments' and 'counter-arguments', you may prefer to present these opposing views in separate paragraphs.

There is no hard and fast rule about the length of paragraphs though it is suggested that varying their length does make the essay more readable. Whatever, don't get hung up about it and concentrate on the content of the essay not the length of paragraphs.

The structure of a paragraph is not a science but a simple rule of consistency that will make sure you stick to the game plan and not waffle on about irrelevant matters. This rule of consistency is in three parts. Normally the opening part of a paragraph will be where you describe the issue or argument that the paragraph will cover. The second part is where you develop this issue or argument, providing a better understanding of what you're talking about. The third part is providing the evidence in relation to the issue or argument.

Writing the concluding paragraph should be the easiest part of your essay. What you have stated in your essay can be pulled together in the conclusion, for example, do the pros outweigh the cons? However, it is seen as beneficial if the conclusion is as thought-provoking as possible. This might include discussing the wider implications of the issue, what might happen if the issue remains unresolved, or what you consider could be done to resolve the issue.

One other simple rule is KEEP IT SIMPLE! Think of books you have read where the author appears to be with you and talking to you. Writing is like talking but in print. When you have thought about what you want to say in your essay, say it as clearly as you can. Keep your sentences as short as possible and read them back to yourself when you've written them to make sure they say what you intended.

Throughout your writing remember that time is of the essence: you only have 30 minutes to write the essay, so keep it concise and accurate.

A final word – there is no doubt that examiners should be more concerned with the content of the essay and not the format, grammar, punctuation and spelling. This may be true but an essay that is pleasing on the eye and easier to read and understand must affect the examiner's approach, even subconsciously. After all they are only human!

21. Critical thinking

This section provides a brief overview of critical thinking, the components of which are useful *per se* but particularly to the TSA Writing Task requirement.

Critical thinking is about how we approach problems, questions and issues, and academicians have suggested it as the best way in which to get at the truth. As already stated earlier in this book, the capacity for critical thought is acknowledged as a valuable intellectual asset in higher education.

Critical thinking is not really a new concept to philosophers and scholars and has actually been around for some time in other guises. For example, in his book *The Improvement of the Mind,* published by Gale and Curtis in 1810, Isaac Watts said:

> Though observation and instruction, reading and conversation, may furnish us with many ideas of men and things, yet it is our own meditation and the labour of our own thought that must form our judgement of things. Our own thoughts should join or disjoin these ideas in a proposition for ourselves: it is our mind that must judge for ourselves concerning the agreement or disagreement of ideas, and form propositions of truth out of them. Reading and conversation may acquaint us with many truths and with many arguments to support them, but it is our own study and reasoning that must determine whether these propositions are true, and whether these arguments are just and solid.

What is critical thinking? Probably the most comprehensive and recent longitudinal study of what constitutes critical thinking was carried out in the USA and Canada. This was a two-year research project involving mainly people in the humanities, sciences, social sciences and educational field. It was conducted on behalf of the American Philosophical Association and the results were published under the title *Critical Thinking: A Statement of Expert Consensus for Purposes of Educational Assessment and Instruction,* The California Academic Press, Millbrae, CA, 1990.

The research identified a number of core critical-thinking skills that include interpretation, analysis, evaluation, inference, explanation and self-regulation, and these are discussed below.

Interpretation

This is about comprehension and expression. It is the ability to be able to understand and give meaning to a wide variety of things, such as a problem, situation, event, rules, procedures, etc.

Analysis

To analyse something we break it down into its constituent parts to see what it actually means. It might be examining ideas or looking for arguments such as identifying what is similar or different between approaches to the solution of a problem. It could also be about identifying unstated assumptions in an article or book.

Evaluation

When we evaluate something we are seeking to establish whether something is credible. This could be judging an author's credibility, comparing the pros and cons of alternative interpretations, or judging whether evidence supports a conclusion.

Inference

This is concerned with the skills of deduction and conclusion. It is the ability to consider information in whatever format and draw from it reasonable conclusions. This might include identifying the implications of advocating a particular position on a subject, or even developing a set of options for addressing a particular problem.

Explanation

Explanation is really self-explanatory! It is the ability to be able to explain the results of one's reasoning. For example, providing the evidence that might have led you to accept or reject a particular position on an issue.

Self-regulation

This is about consciously monitoring what you are doing. For the purposes of the essay it is to be aware of what you are actually writing. You must remain questioning of your biases and personal opinions and assumptions. Really a checking mechanism to reconsider your interpretation or judgement to be sure it is focused on what is required.

The above are considered to be the six cognitive components of critical thinking. A way of encompassing how these skills are used can probably best be demonstrated by considering the effectiveness of solicitors and barristers in our courts. They use reasons to try and convince a judge or jury of a person's guilt or innocence. They evaluate the significance of the evidence presented by the other party and analyse their arguments. They interpret evidence for their client's benefit, make inferences which may or may not be substantiated and give explanation to events or issues. It can be assumed that they are also self-regulating in relation to the protocol required by the court and their own personal biases and beliefs.

Critical thinking is not confined to the cloisters of education but can be characterised by how a person approaches life and living in general. It is something that can be learned and research has shown that there is a significant correlation between critical thinking and reading comprehension. Improvements in critical thinking are paralleled by improvements in reading comprehension.

Chapter 6
Other Oxbridge admissions tests

This section provides information about the other admissions tests required for under-graduate courses at Oxford and Cambridge. The information provided is purely a summary and you are advised to reference the appropriate university website and/or the relevant college for details and requirements.

22. Oxford Tests

Full details of admissions tests and specimen papers for Oxford can be accessed from their website: http://www.ox.ac.uk/admissions/undergraduate_courses/how_to_apply/tests/index.html.

United Kingdom Clinical Aptitude Test (UKCAT)

The United Kingdom Clinical Aptitude Test (UKCAT) is designed to help universities to make more informed choices amongst the many highly qualified applicants who apply for medical and dental degree programmes. The test has been designed to assess those skills, traits and behaviours that identify individuals who will be successful in clinical careers.

The UKCAT is an on-screen examination and has five subtests:

■ **Verbal Reasoning** – assesses your ability to think logically about written information and arrive at a reasoned conclusion – this obviously has similarities with the critical-thinking skills element of the Thinking Skills Assessment.

This subtest comprises 44 items associated with 11 reading passages. Four statements are presented with each passage and there are three answer options for each statement: True, False, or Can't Tell. Twenty-two minutes is allowed for the subtest.

■ **Quantitative Reasoning** – assesses your ability to solve numerical problems and as such is very similar to the problem-solving element of the Thinking Skills Assessment.

This subtest comprises 36 multiple choice questions associated with tables, charts, and/or graphs. Twenty-three minutes is allowed for the subtest and a simple on-screen calculator is available for use during the test.

■ **Abstract Reasoning** – assesses your ability to infer relationships from information by convergent and divergent thinking.

This subtest consists of 65 items associated with 13 pairs of Set A and Set B shapes. Five test shapes are presented with each pair of Set A and Set B shapes and there are three answer options for each test shape: Set A, Set B, or Neither Shape. Sixteen minutes is allowed for the subtest.

■ **Decision Analysis** – assesses your ability to decipher and make sense of coded information.

This subtest consists of one scenario that may contain text, tables and other types of information, and 26 associated items. The items will have four or five response options and for some items more than one of these options may be correct. Thirty-two minutes is allowed for the subtest.

■ **Non-Cognitive Analysis** – assesses attributes and characteristics of robustness, empathy and integrity.

This subtest consists of a series of questions that may vary between 100 and 160 though in any event the time allowed will be 30 minutes. Some questions will be based around a piece of text followed by statements which you will be asked to rate your level of agreement or disagreement with. Some questions will present statements of how you might behave or think in certain situations, and general statements about how you may feel about others. You will be asked to rate the truth or falsity of these statements according to your own beliefs and values. Some questions will present paired statements that represent opposing points of view and you will be asked to indicate your level of agreement on a scale between the two statements. Note that this subtest is currently under review and is not being used as part of the UKCAT.

Biomedical Admissions Test (BMAT)

As with the UKCAT, the BMAT is used for applicants applying for medical and dental degree programmes.

The BMAT has three sections:

■ **Aptitude and Skills** – contains three separate parts: problem solving, understanding argument (critical thinking) and data analysis and influence. This is a multiple-choice question examination of about 22 questions and a total of one hour is allowed.

■ **Scientific Knowledge and Application** – assesses factual scientific and mathematical knowledge at GCSE level. The areas tested include: human biology, cells and cellular structure, basic maths, basic physics equations, and balancing chemical equations. This is a multiple-choice question examination of about 17 questions and a total of 30 minutes is allowed.

■ **Writing Task** – assesses your ability to write a short essay selecting one topic from the three provides and 30 minutes is allowed.

Each of these subtests is in a multiple-choice format and timed separately. The exception is the Non-Cognitive subtest that has no right or wrong answers. This subtest is delivered in less than two hours.

Note: *Passing the UK Clinical Aptitude Test and BMAT* and *Practice Tests, Questions and Answers for the UKCAT* are two books produced by Learning Matters to help you prepare for these admissions tests.

National Admissions Test for Law (LNAT)

The LNAT is a uniform test to be taken by all candidates applying for places on law degrees. Again this admissions test is intended to improve the selection process and to make it fairer to all candidates, irrespective of their educational background. Lawyers – particularly those involved in litigation – spend a significant amount of their time evaluating written assertions and making deductions and conclusions from them. The LNAT is intended to replicate some of the key intellectual competencies required by those wishing to practise law. If students find they are neither stimulated nor attracted by the type of reasoning presented by the LNAT, it may well be that they will not be suited to legal practice.

The LNAT consists of two parts:

- **Section A** – a test designed to assess the verbal reasoning skills at the heart of legal education. The test contains 12 argumentative passages of text followed by between three or four multiple-choice questions containing five options. There are a total of 42 questions and the time allowed for the test is 95 minutes.

- **Section B** – to write a 'well-reasoned' essay on a subject chosen from a list of usually five titles. The time allowed for this part of the test is 40 minutes and the length of the essay should be about 500–600 words.

Note: *Passing the National Admissions Test for Law* is a book produced by Learning Matters to help prepare for this admissions test.

All candidates applying for law degrees must take the LNAT and this is normally sat during September and October. An oral test in the relevant European language is also required of candidates for law with law studies in Europe who are applying for the French, German, Italian or Spanish law options. This test usually takes place in December for those who have been short-listed for interview.

Mathematics Aptitude Test (MAT)

All candidates applying for Mathematics, Mathematics and Statistics, Computer Science, Mathematics and Computer Science, or Mathematics and Philosophy take the MAT. The entrance test is sat in schools, colleges, and test centres and usually takes place in November.

Following the test candidates are shortlisted on the basis of the test score, together with information from applicants' UCAS forms. Interviews at Oxford normally take place in December comprising of about three applicants for each place available.

The test is two-and-a-half hours and examines mathematical knowledge and techniques taken from a syllabus roughly corresponding to the C1 and C2 modules from A-level maths. The syllabus can be found at www.ox.ac.uk/files/imported/prospective students/undergraduate/specimen-test/syllabus.pdf

The MAT consists of two parts:

- a multiple-choice question containing ten parts, each worth four marks, where candidates are encouraged to show their rough workings, although marks are only given for correct answers

- six longer questions, each worth fifteen marks, for which candidates are required to show their workings. Four questions should be attempted, the selection of which depends on the degree for which the candidate is applying.

Extra sheets are included in the booklet for rough work and the use of calculators, formula sheets or dictionaries is prohibited.

English Literature Admissions Test (ELAT)

The ELAT is a pen and paper test of 90 minutes duration and comprises one essay question using two or three passages of text and is taken by all candidates applying to read English at Oxford.

The admissions test will assess how far students have developed their understanding of the key skills of close reading and demonstrating this using unfamiliar material. An explanation of 'close reading' is provided on the Oxford website, viz:

> Close reading has been defined by Elaine Showalter (in *Teaching Literature*, Blackwell: 2003) as 'slow reading, a deliberate attempt to . . . pay attention to language, imagery, allusion, intertextuality, syntax and form.' (p.98) Earlier in the same book she writes: 'The close reading process, or *explication de texte*, that we use in analyzing literary texts does not have to come with the ponderous baggage of the New Criticism, or with political labels. Before or along with attention to factors outside the text, students have to understand something about the verbal, formal, and structural elements of the words themselves.' (p.56)

As the test uses material in the form of poetry and passages that will be unfamiliar to candidates no background reading is required, though the techniques of comparative analysis that form the basis of the assessment can be practised. A sample paper is provided on the website identifying some of the approaches that might be used.

The Writing Task is marked externally with a maximum of 60 marks. The candidates are then banded into four bands – high to low – for the purpose of determining who will be invited for interview. It should be noted that the results of this task is not the only factor in deciding invitations for interview.

Generally, candidates will sit the ELAT at their own school or college, if it is an approved test centre, and other candidates make use of the Open Centre Network. There is no fee for the examination but some open centres may charge an administrative fee for organising and administering the test. The examination is usually scheduled in November.

Physics Aptitude Test (PAT)

The PAT is a two-hour subject-specific admissions test for candidates applying for Physics, and Physics and Philosophy and is normally held in November.

The PAT is conducted at the time of the interview and is in two parts (each part carrying equal weight):

- Part A is about mathematics for physics and contains ten multiple-choice questions;
- Part B is concerned solely with physics and contains ten multiple-choice questions, four questions worth 20 marks requiring written answers, and a long question in five parts worth 20 marks requiring written answers.

All the questions must be attempted and the time allowed for the test is two hours. Calculators, tables or formula may not be used during the test.

As with the ELAT candidates will sit the PAT at their own school or college, if it is an approved test centre, and other candidates make use of the Open Centre Network.

History Aptitude Test (HAT)

The HAT examines the skills and potentialities required for the study of History, and provides an objective basis for comparing candidates. It is used in the selection of candidates for all degree courses involving History, that includes: History (Ancient and Modern); History and Economics (that also requires the Economics Test); History and English (that also requires the ELAT); History and Modern Languages (that also requires the Modern Languages and Linguistics Admissions Tests); History and Politics; and History of Art.

In this test candidates are required to read two extracts (one from a work of History) and answer a total of four questions about them. These questions test comprehension of the arguments contained in the extracts and the candidate's ability to think, make judgements and provide thoughtful interpretations. The HAT is two hours in duration and does not require 'substantive historical knowledge' although candidates are expected to display some historical knowledge to illustrate and develop concepts or hypotheses.

Again, candidates will sit the HAT at their own school or college, if it is an approved test centre, and other candidates make use of the Open Centre Network.

History and Economics Test

The History and Economics Test is for candidates applying for the joint school of History and Economics.

This is a written test that is conducted at the time of interview that is usually held in December. The test comprises one numerical and one critical-reasoning question and candidates are allowed 15 minutes preliminary reading time and 30 minutes for writing.

Fine Art Test

The Fine Art Test is for short-listed candidates and is undertaken at the time of interview, usually in December, at the Ruskin School of Drawing and Fine Art in Oxford.

Candidates are required to make three drawings in any medium, choosing the subject from a list provided at the time of the test. Materials such as paper, card, ink, tape, glue, scissors, pencils and charcoal are provided. There are two examination sessions on the same day, 10.00–12.30 and 1.30–4.00. Subjects may include drawing something within your immediate environment, caricatures, from a piece of written prose, etc.

Psychology, Philosophy and Linguistics Test

This Linguistics Test is used for candidates applying for Psychology and Linguistics and Philosophy and Linguistics courses.

This test is currently under review by Oxford and candidates for these courses are recommended to check the website in relation to any development.

Philosophy Test

The Philosophy Test is used for candidates applying for Philosophy and Theology and Philosophy and Modern Languages and is held at the time of interview, usually in December.

This is a written test and requires the candidates to write two essays, one in relation to the question in Part A, and an essay in relation to one of the three questions contained in Part B. The time allowed for the test is 30 minutes for each essay.

Modern Languages Test

The Modern Languages Test is for all candidates applying for language courses in Czech, French, German, Italian, Modern Greek, Portuguese, Russian or Spanish, and is normally held in November.

The test consists of five questions; question one is in ten parts and questions two to five in five parts. The questions relate to grammar or translation, all the questions must be attempted and 30 minutes is allowed for the test.

Linguistics Test

The Linguistics Test, normally held in November, is for candidates applying for any joint courses involving Linguistics, all joint courses involving Polish (except French with Polish and German with Polish) and all single language courses other than French and German.

This is a pencil and paper test presenting three questions each with a differing number of parts that examines grammar and an invented language. Thirty minutes is allowed for the test and all questions must be answered.

Classics Admissions Test and Classics Language Aptitude Test

The Classics Admissions Test is a one-hour pencil and paper A-Level Standard Test in Latin or Greek requiring candidates to translate Greek or Latin text into English. The test is for short-listed candidates at the time of interview and is usually held in December.

The Classics Language Aptitude Test is a pencil and paper test in three sections, each with a differing number of parts that examines grammar and will probably include an invented language. One hour is allowed for the test and all questions must be answered.

Candidates applying for Classics and English must take the Classics Admissions Test and the English Literature Admissions Test (ELAT), and those applying for Classics and Modern Languages must take the Classics Admissions Test and the Modern Languages and Linguistics Admissions Tests.

Candidates applying for Classics and Oriental Studies who are studying Latin or Greek must take the Classics Admissions Test in the language they are studying and candidates who are studying neither Latin nor Greek to A-level or equivalent must take the Classics Language Aptitude Test.

For candidates who intend to study Arabic, Hebrew, Persian or Turkish as their main language in the first year, the Language Aptitude Test is likely to be in four parts and contain an invented language that will require candidates to give the meaning of or interpret certain phrases. Thirty minutes is allowed for this pencil and paper test. The test will be for short-listed candidates at the time of interview and normally takes place in December.

23. Cambridge Tests

Full details of admissions tests and specimen papers for Oxford can be accessed from their website: http://www.ox.ac.uk/admissions/undergraduate_courses/how_to_apply/tests/index.html

Biomedical Admissions Test (BMAT)

The BMAT is also used by Oxford and details of the test are provided in the previous section.

Sixth Term Examination Paper: Mathematics (STEP)

STEP (Sixth Term Examination Paper) is the mathematics examination used by Cambridge as the basis for unconditional offers. This examination provides a good indication of the candidates' potential, is a useful preparatory tool for the studies that will be undertaken, and the questions contained in STEP are similar to those found in undergraduate mathematics.

STEP consists of three examinations, STEP I, STEP II and STEP III, each of which are three hours in duration, and candidates are usually required to sit either one or two of the examinations. STEP I and STEP II are based on A-level content and STEP III is based on Further Mathematics A-level. STEP III is for candidates studying Further Mathematics. The questions contained in STEP II and STEP III are of the same difficulty but harder than those in STEP I.

Each of the STEP examinations consists of 13 questions comprising: 8 pure mathematics, 3 mechanics and 2 probability and statistics of which candidates choose any 6 questions to answer. Three hours is allowed for each examination. Lined answer sheets and a formula booklet are provided and calculators may not be used. Twenty marks are allocated to each question and the questions that are attempted will also be marked. Where a candidate attempts more than 6 questions all these will be marked but only the best 6 will be used in calculating the final grade. Five grades are used, from 'unclassified' to 'outstanding', and candidates answering 4 questions well are usually awarded a 'very good' grading.

In preparing for the STEP examinations, candidates are advised to attempt the past papers 1998 to 2011 provided on the Cambridge website. The website also contains the STEP specification, list of formulae and statistical tables, information on advanced problems in the mathematics paper, advanced problems in core mathematics, and other website links to help with STEP questions. It also contains the STEP Examiners Report that makes useful reading in relation to common errors made by candidates, for example, ignoring the advice on the front cover of the paper, not being very effective at question-picking, and using time that could have been far better spent tackling another question.

Entries for STEP usually commence in March with a final closing date of May. All three papers are set on different dates, normally during June, and the results are released in August. Generally, candidates will sit the STEP at their own school or college if it is an approved test centre, and other candidates make use of the Open Centre Network. Details of Open Centres can be found on the Cambridge website together with the fees for the examinations.

Cambridge Law Test

This is a recently new test being used by Cambridge who previously, like Oxford, used the National Admissions Test for Law (LNAT). According to the Cambridge website the test 'is intended to complement the other elements of our admissions process, such as interviews, and consideration of academic performance to date, and the terms of conditional offers.'

The paper-based test is taken by all applicants at the time of interview and requires them to answer one question in one hour. Although the questions are law-based candidates are assured that prior knowledge of the law is not required. All of the information required to answer the questions is provided in the passage and you are assured that previous students of law will not be at an advantage. Specimen questions are available on the Cambridge website and may be of three types: essay, problem-solving or comprehension questions. Obviously, it is recommended that you familiarise yourself with the questions and determine appropriate answers.